T0279647

THE
ROFFIGNAC

THE
ROFFIGNAC

ROBERT F. MOSS

LOUISIANA STATE UNIVERSITY PRESS
BATON ROUGE

Published by Louisiana State University Press
lsupress.org

Copyright © 2024 by Robert F. Moss

Manufactured in the United States of America
First printing

Designer: Barbara Neely Bourgoyne
Typeface: Arno Pro
Printer and binder: Integrated Books International

Cover photograph courtesy Sam Gregory Anselmo.

Cataloging-in-Publication Data are available at the Library of Congress.

ISBN 978-0-8071-8262-8 (cloth)

for John Shelton Reed

CONTENTS

ACKNOWLEDGMENTS

More than a decade ago, the late Tom Freeland of Oxford, Mississippi, connected me with Tom Fitzmorris, proprietor of the indispensable New Orleans Menu website, author of *Hungry Town,* and coauthor of the *Lost Restaurants of New Orleans.* Fitzmorris, in turn, shared his memories of the Roffignac cocktail from his days dining at Maylie's back in the 1970s, as well as the recipe from the old Maylie's menu, which proved invaluable to my search.

I am indebted to prior researchers and writers who have uncovered important pieces of the Roffignac story, too, most notably James Karst and Errol Laborde. Thanks to Chris Hannah at the Jewel of the South for the tasty Roffignac and engaging conversation. The staff at the Reading Room of the Historic New Orleans Collection was welcoming and very helpful.

Neal Bodenheimer of Cure, Peychaud's, and Dauphine's went above and beyond in hosting me for a Roffignac tasting session at Cure and giving me a wealth of ideas to ponder when it comes to drink construction and historical recreations.

Jenny Keegan, Neal Novak, freelance copyeditor Lee Sioles, and the entire team at the LSU Press helped take a rough, somewhat rambling tale and transform it into a polished book.

Finally, many thanks are due to John Shelton Reed, a great friend and kindred spirit, who made me aware of the Iconic New Orleans Cocktails series and helped get yet another book project of mine off the ground. Who knew that a single lunch at Hominy Grill would have such a payoff?

THE
ROFFIGNAC

INTRODUCTION

IN SEARCH OF THE ROFFIGNAC

On my last visit to New Orleans, I snagged a stool at the white stone–topped bar at Peychaud's and ordered a Roffignac. I watched as the bartender picked up a double-ended jigger and measured out a dose of clear liquor and a dose of pink raspberry shrub and topped the mixture with soda water.

The finished drink was pale pink in hue, and it was placed in front of me in a low-stemmed glass garnished with two pristine red raspberries speared on a golden pick.

The Roffignac at Peychaud's. Photograph courtesy of the author.

The clear liquor, the menu told me, was Cobrafire Eau de Vie de Raisin, a 102.6 proof unaged white brandy from the Armagnac region in France. The first sip was delightful, a little fruity with some minty notes, but still quite boozy. The cocktail's icy sweetness really hit the spot after a long stroll through the steamy French Quarter.

It was a delicious drink, and a beautiful one, too. And I already knew it didn't bear even a passing resemblance to a nineteenth-century Roffignac.

A SLOW REVIVAL

The Roffignac has long been the most mysterious of New Orleans's many signature cocktails. In the decades just before Prohibition, travel writers routinely placed it alongside the Ramos Gin Fizz, the Sazerac, and the Absinthe Frappé in lists of the city's must-try beverages. Unlike those other drinks, the Roffignac barely survived Prohibition, and it faded to near-extinction in the decades that followed.

Here in the twenty-first century, most of the classic New Orleans cocktail canon has been reclaimed and revitalized, thanks in large part to the craft cocktail movement. Bartenders of a historical bent have dug into old bar manuals and newspaper archives and unearthed a wealth of detail about those drinks' origins. Even if the stories conflict (and many do) or the precise ingredients and proportions are debated (some hotly so), we've managed to recreate contemporary versions of the old classics that taste delicious and seem relatively close to the originals.

The Roffignac has proven a tougher nut to crack. It is widely agreed that the drink was named in honor of Joseph Roffignac, a French immigrant who served as mayor of New Orleans from 1820 to 1828. How and when it received that name has remained a mystery. It is clear that the Roffignac had emerged as one of the city's signature drinks by the 1890s, when many references to it appear in newspapers and magazines. Travel guides from the period tell us Mannessier's Confectionery on Royal Street was particularly famous for its Roffignacs. The drink lingered on through the twentieth century at Maylie's Restaurant on Poydras Street, where it remained the house cocktail until the restaurant closed in 1986. By that point it had been forgotten everywhere else.

Eventually, after resurrecting such obscure classics as the Last Word and the Brandy Crusta, the revivalists of pre-Prohibition cocktails turned their attention to the Roffignac. Around 2010, recipes for the drink began popping up on various cocktail enthusiast blogs. Almost all drew from a single source: Stanley Clisby Arthur's *Famous New Orleans Drinks and How to Mix 'Em*, a slim 1937 volume that had become a popular resource for those digging into the New Orleans classics. The Roffignac, Arthur relates, was named for Joseph Roffignac (a.k.a. Count Louis Philippe Joseph de Roffignac), a nobleman who fled his native country during the French Revolution, fought the British under Andrew Jackson at the Battle of New Orleans, and became a state legislator and mayor of New Orleans. Along with that back story, Arthur provides a recipe:

| 1 jigger whiskey | Seltzer or soda water |
| 1 pony sirup | Raspberry sirup |

Pour into a highball glass the jigger of whiskey [or use cognac, as in the original drink]. Add the sirup, which may be raspberry, grenadine, or red Hembarig, the sweetening used in New Orleans a century ago. Add the soda water. Ice, of course.

"Jigger" and "pony" refer to the two sides of a standard double-sided cocktail measuring cup, the jigger holding 1.5 ounces and the pony 1 ounce. "Sirup" would be what we call simple syrup today—equal volumes of water and sugar boiled together into a thick, clear syrup.

Arthur's notes to the recipe offer a few extra nuggets, including the explanation that the curious-sounding "red Hembarig" was "a popular sirup when old New Orleans was young." This detail threw cocktail revivalists for a loop (myself included), for no one could find a trace of a syrup called "hembarig," red or otherwise, in any source besides Arthur's book. We took stabs at making the cocktail with grenadine and raspberry syrup but struggled to come up with a palatable mixture, much less something that might rival the Sazerac or the Ramos Gin Fizz. The secret, we concluded, must be in that mysterious red Hembarig, if we could only figure out what it was.

The answer, many surmised, must lie in the past, when "old New Orleans was young." Arthur states only that the Roffignac cocktail was "linked" with the popular mayor but doesn't explain how or when it originated. So what was this Roffignac cocktail, anyway, and why has its story been so hard to pin down?

RED HEMBARIG AND RED HERRINGS

I took a stab at explaining the origins of the Roffignac cocktail in my book *Southern Spirits: 400 Years of Drinking in the American South* (2016), in which I declared that the Roffignac first appeared on the scene at Mannessier's in the 1890s. I also published a recipe for "The Original (Perhaps) Roffignac Cocktail" that began with 1½ ounces of cognac. I was wrong on both counts.

To date, the writer who has come closest to cracking the case is James Karst, who in a 2016 story for the *Times-Picayune* traces the cocktail back to a drugstore ad in 1874. Karst hypothesizes that the drink may not have been named for the famous mayor but rather "was simply a popular drink made with Roffignac cognac, not unlike the way the Sazerac took its name from the brandy that was a main ingredient." This, it turns out, is not the case, either. (In fact, it's not even certain that brandy was ever a "main ingredient" in a Sazerac cocktail, but that's a debate for another day.)

One thing that trips us up when searching for the Roffignac's origins is that we tend to make a lot of assumptions based upon common conceptions of New Orleans's dining and drinking history as well as popular images of the city. Its roots as a French and Spanish colony are among the city's most distinctive characteristics, and writers have a natural tendency to superimpose gauzy myths of French Creoles onto any treatment of nineteenth-century New Orleans. Equally appealing are tales of swashbuckling pirates and the exploits of Andrew Jackson during the Battle of New Orleans in the War of 1812. If storytellers can find a way to work Frenchmen, Old Hickory, and pirates into the same narrative, they've hit the trifecta. Just witness the many tales of the pirate Jean Lafitte and Andrew Jackson meeting in 1814 over drinks in the Old Absinthe House on Bourbon Street to plan the defense of New Orleans. (Never mind that the building housed a grocery store at the time.)

In the case of the Roffignac, right out of the gate we have a French-born mayor from the 1820s, and the gravitational pull of that detail drags the story back toward the early decades of the nineteenth century. Little wonder that so many commentators have concluded that the beverage must have originated during the Roffignac administration and perhaps was even invented by the mayor himself.

Others have asked whether the mayor is a red herring. Karst is not the only one to notice Arthur's statement that the original drink used cognac and wonder whether the Roffignac might actually have been named for a cognac brand. There was (and still is) a Roffignac cognac—Comte Ferdinand de Roffignac Cognac, to be precise—and the cocktail indeed has a linkage to that brand, but, as we will see, that connection is rather serpentine and runs in the opposite direction from what these commentators assume.

When most writers today refer to the Roffignac, they call it a "cocktail." In fact, the very book you are reading is published in a series called "Iconic New Orleans Cocktails." That term links it with the many other alcoholic creations that emerged from the city's nineteenth-century bars, which were usually called coffeehouses or cabarets back then. The fact that the last syllable of the name echoes that of cognac and Sazerac further suggests that the Roffignac must have been born in a bar. Errol Laborde, writing in *New Orleans* magazine in 2019, proceeds down that exact path. "Served with ice in an Old Fashion glass," he writes, "the drink is a local version of the genre of slow slipping cocktails. In an age when the male work force spent many hours both during and after work propped against a bar, the Roffignac seemed to have its following."

If we're searching for the Roffignac in a nineteenth-century bar, though, we're looking in the wrong place, especially if that establishment is patronized primarily by "the male work force." As it turns out, there were many other places one could get an alcoholic drink in nineteenth-century New Orleans, and the Roffignac came from one of those alternative venues. It's not surprising that the origins of the Roffignac are murky, for the cocktail began deliberately as a means of deception. Conceived in subterfuge and born in New Orleans, it never strayed far from the city. Technically it was not even a cocktail, though it certainly packed a sneaky punch.

On one level, this book tells the story of how this once-famous drink came to be and how it almost disappeared in the twentieth century. At the same time, it maps out the larger story of drinking and recreation in nineteenth-century New Orleans and how they evolved over time. The drink's history highlights the central role that narrative has always played in our cocktail culture, and how slippery and unreliable those stories can sometimes be.

And, yes, we're bound to turn up a recipe or two along the way.

CHAPTER ONE

WHO WAS COUNT ROFFIGNAC?

To uncover the story of the Roffignac we must first establish the context in which it was born. And before we do that, we need to address the cocktail's namesake, Mayor Roffignac, and determine what role, if any, he plays in the story.

The details of Joseph Roffignac's life are murky, which is only fitting for the man who lent his name to such a mysterious beverage. His biography is riddled with gaps and missing pieces, and various writers over the years have made questionable suppositions or indulged in romantic embellishments when trying to pull the threads together. Still, the facts that can be verified sketch the outlines of a remarkable life of adventure and achievement that ultimately ended in sadness.

Count Louis-Philippe Joseph de Roffignac was born into a noble family in 1773 at Angoulême in the Périgord region of southwestern France. His father, Count René-Anibal de Roffignac, was a captain in the Regiment of Chartres, and at the age of 17 Joseph received a commission as a lieutenant of artillery. It wasn't great timing, for revolutionary fervor was sweeping France. By the time King Louis XVI was executed in 1793 and the Reign of Terror descended, Joseph and his father, as well as his two brothers, had all fled the country and become naturalized citizens of Spain.

The elder Count Roffignac became field marshal of the Spanish armies and fought against the forces of the revolutionary Republic of France. He died in Madrid in 1807. Young Joseph, like many French emigres, made his way to North America, though when and where he arrived is uncertain. By the early 1800s, he had found his way to the

Spanish colony of West Florida, where he served as a captain in the Dragoons of Mexico.

The Louisiana Purchase of 1803 made New Orleans and the land south and west of the Mississippi River part of the young United States. Not included in the deal were the so-called Florida Parishes, a stretch of land that included Baton Rouge and was bounded on the north by the 31st parallel (now the Mississippi state line) and on the south by Lake Pontchartrain. In the fall of 1804 Roffignac led a detachment of fifty dragoons from Pensacola to Baton Rouge to defend Spain's Fort San Carlos from unruly and acquisitive Americans, who were increasingly moving southward and settling in what was still Spanish-held territory. While in the area, Roffignac began buying up tracts of land in and around Baton Rouge. He further advanced his fortunes in 1806 when he married Solidelle de Montégut, the daughter of Dr. Joseph Montégut, former chief surgeon of the Spanish royal hospital and a significant landowner in New Orleans. The union was accompanied by a $10,000 dowry, paid by Dr. Montégut.

Count Louis-Philippe Joseph de Roffignac. Courtesy Historic New Orleans Collection, 1984.115.22 i–viii.

On September 23, 1810, a party of armed Americans stormed Fort San Carlos, killed two Spanish soldiers, and declared the short-lived independent Republic of West Florida. Just two months later, President James Madison ordered the Florida Parishes to be absorbed into the Orleans Territory, insisting, on dubious grounds, that the land had been part of the Louisiana Purchase all along. In 1812, those parishes entered the union along with the rest of Louisiana as the 18th American state.

FROM SOLDIER TO MAYOR

Whether the future mayor had any involvement in the so-called West Florida Rebellion is unknown. Sometime during those transition years, Joseph Roffignac, having long before dropped his royal title, left the Spanish army and settled in New Orleans. Records from the period spell his last name in various ways, including Rouffignac, Rofignac, Rofiniac, and even Roufigniaco. In the governmental records of Spanish West Florida, he appears frequently as

José Roffignac. In the 1820s, however, his official mayoral notices in the local newspapers were consistently signed "J. Roffignac," which we can assume was his preferred spelling.

Few details survive about Roffignac's early years in New Orleans. Later biographical accounts claim he served as a colonel in the Louisiana Legion during the War of 1812, but that volunteer militia unit was not formed until 1821. Despite his long career in the Spanish army, there is no evidence that Roffignac served in any American militia unit nor that, as Stanley Clisby Arthur would later claim, he "fought under 'Old Hickory' in the Battle of New Orleans." Roffignac did, however, become actively involved in business ventures and local politics. In 1812 he was elected to represent Orleans Parish in the newly formed Louisiana House of Representatives, serving a total of six terms. In 1818, he was appointed to the first board of directors of the new Louisiana State Bank. That same year he threw his hat into the ring for mayor of New Orleans, finishing last of the four candidates. Roffignac tried again in 1820 and this time won handily, with 527 votes against his two competitors'

388 and 112. He would be re-elected three times and serve four consecutive two-year terms.

Most historians portray Roffignac as an effective and popular mayor. He was among the first leaders to recognize the city's rising commercial potential, and he took strides to prepare for future growth. His administration undertook measures to clean and better police the streets and to improve the public squares, including planting sycamores and elms in the Place d'Armes (now Jackson Square) and along Esplanade, Rampart, and Canal streets. Roffignac awarded the city's first contract for paving its muddy streets, which was accomplished by laying down cobblestones and covering them with a layer of sand and gravel. Prior to Roffignac's administration, the streets were pitch black after nightfall, and citizens had to carry lanterns for even short outings. The mayor oversaw the installation of a regular system of lighting, which consisted of large lamps with reflectors that were suspended high above the streets by long ropes stretching from posts at each corner.

These efforts came at a cost, though, and more conservative New Orleanians accused the Roffignac administration of extravagance, for the mayor was willing to take on debt to pay for civic improvements. His administration faced numerous other challenges, too, for the 1820s were a rough-and-tumble period for the small but rapidly growing city. As internal improvements opened the Ohio and Mississippi for navigation and trade, a never-ending influx of strangers swarmed into town. Hundreds of barges and flatboats arrived each day bearing flour, grain, and cured beef to sell. Licensed gambling was permitted in the city, and the gambling dens as well as the coffeehouses, barrooms, and brothels were open all night. Drunken brawls broke out regularly and, with only a small police force, assaults and robberies were rife.

Roffignac reorganized the "gens d'armes," a part of the police force, and pushed to better organize and expand what were then volunteer fire companies, but public order remained an ongoing problem. His crowning moment as mayor occurred in April 1825, when the Marquis de Lafayette made his famed visit to New Orleans and Roffignac greeted the Revolutionary war hero with a speech under a great arch in the Place d'Armes.

When Roffignac stepped down as mayor at the end of his fourth term, the city council passed a resolution praising him for "zeal in executing the laws, and in maintaining public order" and for his "well designated plans of improvements." In his response, Roffignac expressed that he was "deeply impressed with the importance of this rising city" and declared that "slow and gradual progress did not comport with the spirits of the times, and did not accord with the wishes of an enterprising population." That enterprising population had indeed grown under Roffignac's watch, increasing from 27,176 in 1820 to 46,082 in 1830. It would keep growing, too, more than doubling during the 1830s to reach 102,193 in 1840, making New Orleans the third largest city in the country, behind only Baltimore and New York.

By that point, though, the mayor was gone. On June 13, 1828, the ship *Meridian* sailed from New Orleans, bound for Bordeaux, with thirty-two passengers aboard, one of whom was Joseph Roffignac. The former mayor had reportedly inherited a sizeable estate from an aunt, and with the French Revolution and the Napoleonic Era now past and the Bourbon monarchy restored, he was going home to reclaim his family's old property. Though he declared his intention to return to New Orleans in the future, he never saw the city again.

TOO LATE TO GO BACK

Around 1845, the Louisiana politician and historian Charles Gayarré visited Roffignac at his chateau near the town of Périgueux. Now approaching 80 years old, the former mayor, Gayarré recalled, "tenderly welcomed me, pressed me in his arms, but, alas!, wept bitterly." As they spoke, Gayarré could see that life for Roffignac "had become . . . an insupportable burden. He deplored that he had ever left Louisiana, which had become his real home, while his native country had ceased in his eye to retain that character after such a lapse of time. Now it was too late—too late to go back!"

In October of 1846, the *Times-Picayune* published a shocking piece of news received via letter from Paris. "Mr. Roffignac, formerly Mayor of this city," the brief notice states, "recently committed suicide at his residence near Angouleme, France. The cause for the rash act is not known."

Of course, it wouldn't be a proper Roffignac tale without some final intrigue, and the story of the former mayor's death took on more color over time. When Count Yves de Roffignac, the great nephew of Joseph Roffignac, visited New Orleans in 1893, the *Times-Picayune* took the occasion to publish a profile of the former mayor and his accomplishments. "Unfortunately for the city," the account concluded, "old Roffignac went to Paris . . . and while doing some target practice with a pistol was accidentally shot."

Two years later, Henry C. Castellanos offered a more detailed and contradictory account in his capsule biography of Roffignac in *New Orleans as It Was* (1895). The former mayor, Castellanos explains, had been suffering from a chronic disease for some time. While "resting in his invalid's arm-chair" and loading a pistol, "he was suddenly stricken down by an apoplectic attack. Just as he was about to fall the pistol was discharged and several small buck shots lodged behind his ear." Castellanos admits that "these circumstances of a peculiar character . . . gave at first to the supposition that he had committed suicide," but he then asserts, "a medical examination at once dispelled the suspicion." Subsequent writers picked up on Castellanos's account, and that unlikely explanation for the mayor's death is repeated to this day.

No, the popular Mayor Roffignac did not invent the cocktail that bears his name, nor did he ever taste one. By the time we find the first trace of a beverage called a Roffignac, the mayor had been dead for more than twenty years. There's good reason why one might name a cocktail after Joseph Roffignac, though. For starters, his story and his melodic name have a touch of mystery and romance about them. The name also shares its ending syllable with cognac and armagnac, two prized types of French brandy that have long been associated with New Orleans. It offers echoes of Sazerac, too, that famed red-hued cocktail. More than anything, a Roffignac just sounds like something you might drink in New Orleans.

CHAPTER TWO

SETTING THE SCENE

Before we go looking for the original Roffignac, we need to understand its native habitat. The drink, after all, was not invented out of whole cloth in a flash of inspiration. It emerged from a convergence of social and commercial trends in New Orleans, and the city's dining and drinking culture changed dramatically between the time when Joseph Roffignac was mayor and the moment when the beverage named for him first appeared on the scene.

LET'S GET A DRINK

Our first order of business is to find ourselves a drink, and there were plenty of places where one could do that in mid nineteenth-century New Orleans. "There is perhaps no city in this country," the *Daily Picayune* declared in 1848, "where the bar-rooms are constructed upon so extensive a scale as in New Orleans. They are scattered in all directions, in every quarter of the city, and are of all sorts, from the miserable 'picayune groggery' to the magnificent 'dime house.'" Those terms refer to the price of the drinks at each type of establishment, for a picayune (originally a Spanish coin worth half a real, or 6.25 cents) was a popular term for a nickel. A dime was the standard price for a cocktail at the more upscale coffeehouses.

By the early nineteenth century, the coffeehouse (a.k.a. café) was an entrenched New Orleans institution. Though it traced its lineage to Parisian cafés and London coffee houses, in New Orleans the term was always something of a misnomer. "Though their usual denomination is 'coffeehouse,'" observed Joseph Holt Ingraham, who visited the city in the 1830s, "they have no earthly, whatever may be their spiritual, right to such a distinction; it is merely a 'nomme de profession.'" A coffeehouse tended to be extravagantly decorated with large mirrors, expensive carpets, and costly glassware. The walls were usually bedecked with nude portraits of angels or, as one local newspaper put it in 1850, "the nude daughters of those who are 'but little lower than the angels.'" Within that lush if somewhat gaudy setting, the preferred drinks were imported brandy, "sangaree" (sangria), and "negus"—port wine mixed with water, sugar, and spices. Patrons passed the time reading their newspapers, playing dominos, and puffing on cigars.

One visitor to New Orleans estimated there were a hundred coffeehouses in operation in the city in the 1830s. Many of these establishments took on the name "exchange," for New Orleans's coffeehouses were as much places to conduct business in as they were to drink and socialize. The Exchange Coffee House was perhaps the most famous, and Hewlett's Exchange, the Merchant's Exchange, and the

New Commercial Exchange were popular destinations in the 1840s and 1850s.

Similar in scale and grandeur were the barrooms at the city's leading hotels. The octagonal bar in the basement of the St. Charles Hotel was commonly called the St. Charles Exchange, and its counterpart at the rival St. Louis Hotel in the French quarter was known as the St. Louis Exchange. Both offered free lunches to draw in daytime customers. Louis Fitzgerald Taistro, who visited New Orleans in the early 1840s, noted that every day between the hours of eleven and noon, merchants and their clerks would race from their offices, "each and all wending their way to some of the great refectories, where, by paying a solitary 'bit' (tenpence of New-York money) for liquor . . . you are allowed to partake of as sumptuous a fare as ever graced the table of a titled epicure."

The St. Charles Exchange offered the most elaborate spread. "The room occupies the ground floor of the hotel," Taistro wrote, "and is capable of accommodating from four to five hundred persons without inconvenience." The sixty-foot bar was "crowded with hungry disputants, before whom were displayed all the delicacies of the season and out of season, from turtle soup, wild turkey, and hot venison, down to calves feet *á la vinaigrette, paté de foie gras,* and *macaroni ail fromage gratté.*"

Lower down the scale from a coffeehouse or hotel bar was the cabaret. In colonial New Orleans that term had been the equivalent to the English tavern, meaning a place that not only served drinks but also provided meals and lodging for travelers. By the 1840s, the lodging functions had largely fallen away, and New Orleans cabarets had become primarily drinking establishments. More modest and plainly furnished than coffeehouses, they tended to be located in corner buildings on residential blocks, with the owners and their families often living in back rooms or on the second floor. Many were run by immigrants, and their patrons tended to be of the same national origins as the owner. French and Spanish cabarets featured imported wines, cordials, anisette, absinthe, and cognac, while German-run ones stocked beer, schnapps, and cheap German wines. Irish and Anglo-American establishments, which were often attached to grocery stores, were more diverse in their offerings, serving everything from fine wines and cognac to cheap porter and whiskey. Rarely found in these middle-tier houses were what we would today call cocktails. "Mint juleps, punches, cobblers, smashes, and such fancy condiments," the *Daily Picayune* noted in 1850, "are made principally in the coffee-houses. . . . In the cabaret the liquor preferred is called for, quickly drunk and the customer is off with but little tarrying."

Lowest in status were the city's groggeries and tippling houses, which were sometimes licensed businesses or a sideline for boarding house keepers. Many, though, were unlicensed operations run from people's homes or in conjunction with a brothel, and they dispensed cheap liquor by the drink, and little else. In one of his semi-annual reports in 1852, the chief of police noted that there were more than 1,300 establishments selling spirituous liquors in New Orleans, and some 500 of them were unlicensed. Newspapers from that decade are filled with reports of citizens— many of them women—being charged with selling liquor by the drink without a license. Also common in the court reports are persons charged with keeping "a disorderly tippling house," including two men whose operations were described as "the resorts of the vilest of humanity," and one Mrs. Green, whose tippling house was "the resort of lewd and abandoned women."

As diverse as they were in size and sophistication, there was one characteristic that the city's coffeehouses, barrooms, and cabarets all shared: their patrons were almost exclusively male. Public drinking establishments were highly gendered spaces in the nineteenth century, in New Orleans as well as the rest of the country. Though many women owned and operated cabarets and tippling houses, there was great social stigma against "respectable ladies" being seen drinking in them, lest they be judged "lewd and abandoned women."

By the 1850s, the patrons were almost exclusively white, too. The selling of alcohol to enslaved persons had long been forbidden, and any free persons of color found mingling with enslaved persons in a cabaret could also be fined. As white fears of disorder and rebellions heightened in the 1850s, the city moved to prohibit the sale of alcohol to all persons of color, free or enslaved. The proprietors of neighborhood cabarets and tippling houses often flouted those laws, though, and the court records from the period are filled with cases of defendants being charged with selling liquor by the drink to enslaved people.

THE RISE OF THE SODA FOUNTAIN

Not every New Orleanian seeking a refreshing beverage wanted booze in it. The soda fountain plays a central role in the Roffignac story, and over the course of the nineteenth century, the apparatus and beverages it dispensed evolved from a quirky novelty to a staple of the city's amusement scene.

Long before soda fountains existed, Europeans and Americans had been drinking the effervescent waters that bubbled up naturally from mineral springs, to which they often attributed mystical healing qualities. In the 1770s, chemists in Europe, including the noted British scientist Joseph Priestley, began experimenting with infusing ordinary water with carbon dioxide, or "fixed air," as it was termed at the time. Their goal was to simulate the mineral-rich waters of famous European springs so they could be manufactured locally for a fraction of the cost of transporting them from the springs themselves. Building upon Priestley's work, John Mervin Nooth created and published the designs for an improved carbonation apparatus. British apothecaries quickly adopted Nooth's devices and began manufacturing and selling "artificial waters" in their shops, marketing them initially for medicinal usage. By the turn of the nineteenth century, England enjoyed a thriving trade in soda and imitation mineral waters, which were produced on a large scale in factories and sold through retail shops in returnable bottles.

A market quirk caused the soda water industry to develop along very different lines in the young United States. Unlike in England, glassware in America was expensive and of generally poor quality, and that limitation led to a rise of a different type of retail outlet: the soda fountain. In 1806 Benjamin Silliman, a professor of chemistry at Yale, imported a Nooth apparatus and began manufacturing artificial mineral water, but he struggled to obtain glass or stoneware vessels that wouldn't burst under the confined gas's pressure. Silliman and his partners decided to open a shop in New Haven instead, where they sold water drawn directly from fountains and served in glasses for on-premise consumption. The venture proved a success, and the partners took the idea to New York City, where they installed soda fountains in the City Hotel and the popular Tontine Coffeehouse. Rival vendors soon opened shops of their own, and fountains quickly began popping up in other northeastern cities. By 1812, *The Emporium of Arts and Sciences* reported, "the use of artificial Mineral Waters" had become "very general in our large cities, both as a medicine and a luxury."

In early fountains, the generating apparatus was usually housed in the basement beneath the serving room. An operator below would create carbon dioxide in an enclosed vessel by dissolving pieces of chalk or marble in diluted sulfuric acid and then using a manual pump to saturate water in a separate tank with the gas. The resulting pressure raised the now-carbonated water through a block tin tube to the dispensing fountain in the room above. Atop the bar or serving counter, the dispensing tubes were hidden inside decorative mahogany pillars topped with gilded urns. Over time, fountain operators took to chilling the water by passing the tubes through large tubs of ice, so the product emerged from the fountain crisply cold and fizzy.

That chilling process was essential for making soda water a refreshing summertime beverage, and it's fitting that the product first appeared in New Orleans in connection with the city's first ice dealer. Ice had always been rare in the lower South during winter and completely unavailable the rest of the year, for there was no means of mechanical refrigeration until after the Civil War. In the first decades of the nineteenth century, however, a series of enterprising pioneers established a coastwide ice trade. They arranged to have giant blocks of ice carved from northern lakes in the spring, loaded onto ships, and delivered to southern ports. There the blocks would be stored in rudimentary icehouses, insulated with sawdust and similar materials, in hopes that enough could be sold to turn a profit before the inventory melted away.

In 1819, Richard Salmon established the first icehouse in New Orleans, near the basin of the old Canal Carondelet just north of the French Quarter. By July he was distributing ice in pails to subscribers who had purchased tickets to fund the first shipment. As a side business, he operated what he called a Liquid Magnesia and Mineral Water store on Royal Street. Salmon had licensed the patent from Dr. Cullen of Philadelphia for "solution of magnesia" (that is, magnesium hydroxide), which he promised would "compose" the stomach, allay vomiting, and carry off "Bile and offensive matter." It was, in plain words, a laxative—a forerunner of the product called Milk of Magnesia. Alongside the magnesia solution, Salmon also sold soda water "securely bottled" for $2.25 per dozen bottles. Salmon's icehouse and the associated mineral water store lasted only a single season. Several other entrepreneurs launched similar unsuccessful ventures during the 1820s, but it wasn't until E. Serreau established the New Orleans Ice House on Chartres Street in 1829 that the city had access to a reliable supply of ice.

Artificial mineral water became more widely available

during this period, too. By 1820 C. Stevenson had opened a shop on Chartres Street, where he sold soda water and imitation Saratoga, Ballston, Epsom, and Rochelle waters (all famous springs), imported in casks from New York. Later in the decade, Stevenson added a fountain and begin producing his own waters. In 1822, a rival dealer named S. B. Duplantier established what he termed "a manufactory of mineral waters" on St. Louis Street, just three doors from the levee. There he kept a mineral water fountain selling a glass of soda or Seltzer water, plain or flavored with a syrup, for six and a quarter cents.

Up to this point, artificial waters were still promoted primarily as medicinal cure-alls. Soda water, Duplantier claimed in his advertisements, had been found effective in treating "gouty or rheumatic affections" and provided relief for strangury, acidity of the stomach, and indigestion. He touted Seltzer water—an imitation of the waters from natural springs in Seltzer, Germany—for treating "affections of the lungs" and "feverish irritations" as well as generally soothing and strengthening the stomach.

Tufts Soda-Water Fountain advertisement, 1878.

Soda dealers soon found they could sell more water if, instead of simply imitating the mineral taste of natural springs, they began flavoring it with various roots, herbs, and fruit-flavored syrups. The flavoring of soda water and the development of smaller, less expensive fountains helped push the beverage from the world of medicine to the world of confectionery and other pleasurable indulgences. Though apothecary shops and specialized soda retailers remained popular places to acquire fizzy water, soda fountains could increasingly be found in all sorts of amusement venues.

When Bevan & Williamson opened the Rising Sun and Auction Coffee Room on Chartres Street in 1828, they announced not only that "their bar will be furnished with the best of liquors" but also that they had "erected a Soda Fountain, for the accommodation of their customers." In 1838, the owners of the St. Charles Theatre announced that for the summer months they were launching "Vauxhall In the St. Charles Theatre," a reference to the famed London pleasure garden. The orchestra pit would be covered over and transformed into a "fanciful garden," and each evening guests could stroll among flowered bowers, fountains, and grottos while enjoying musical entertainment, dramatic performances, ice creams, and soda water supplied by one Mr. Nichols. By 1848, as the *Picayune* noted in a feature on summer beverages, "soda fountains [were] fizzing away in all directions and disseminating their gaseous contents along avenues of thirsty throats."

SODA SYRUPS

The flavoring syrups used by soda fountain operators turn out to be a key part of the Roffignac story. Early soda water dealers prided themselves on making their own "sirups," as it was often spelled. As the soda fountain business developed, an increasing number of firms popped up to supply pre-made syrups to the trade. This growth was made possible by the decreasing cost of sugar, a trend in which Louisiana played an active role, for the state became the center of American sugar production in the early nineteenth century.

We should note that the sugar produced on Louisiana plantations was not the pure white crystals we know today. It was still a rather rough article produced by methods little different from those used during the colonial era, only on a larger scale. Even the most refined form—so-called "loaf sugar," which was packed into cone-shaped molds and lightened with a white clay slurry—contained a considerable amount of molasses and therefore had a much darker flavor than the near-pure sucrose of modern granulated sugar.

In his 1862 *Manual for the Manufacture of Cordials, Liquors, Fancy Syrups, & C.*, Professor Christian Schultz provided instructions on how to "Clarify Loaf-Sugar and make Syrup." The process begins by breaking the sugar cones into small pieces in a copper pan, adding a pint of water for every pound of sugar, beating in egg whites, and then boiling the mixture over a fire. The syrup maker skimmed the syrup as it boiled, adding cold water several times and returning it to a boil, until no more scum rose to the surface. The syrup was then strained through a fine cloth or flannel sieve, leaving it "extra fine and clear."

This base of so-called simple syrup could be flavored by adding fruit, fruit juices, roots, or herbs. The most popular early fruit flavors were lemon, raspberry, strawberry, and pineapple, while ginger and sarsaparilla (the root of a woody vine native to tropical rainforests) were the most common herbal flavorings. Because fresh fruit was expensive and syrups made from them didn't keep very long, many druggists and syrup manufacturers began using artificial flavorings like citric acid to mimic the bite of citrus and tincture of orris root to simulate the flavor of raspberries.

Soda drinkers in New Orleans had another preferred flavor for their soda water. In its 1848 article on summer beverages, the *Picayune* had noted that, "the mead founts pour out their grateful meed of acknowledgement to the thirsty public for the favor of the warm weather." Traditional mead is a beer-like alcoholic beverage brewed from fermented honey. The soda fountain version was made with a nonalcoholic syrup akin to sarsaparilla or root beer. Nineteenth-century recipes for mead syrup (or, New Orleans Mead, as it was often called) start with a base of sugar syrup, honey, and water that is flavored with an array of spices, including mace, cloves, cinnamon, ginger, nutmeg, sassafras, and tonka beans. Mead-flavored soda was found in New Orleans by at least 1827, when John Clark advertised for sale "a complete apparatus for making soda water and carbonated mead with four fountains." By the 1830s, multiple soda shops in New Orleans—including those of N. Holmes on St. John Street and Nicholl's on Camp Street—were advertising mead alongside plain soda water, and more followed in the 1840s.

THE SECRETS OF
RED HEMBARIG REVEALED

New Orleanians, then, had no shortage of options for flavoring their beverages at soda fountains. But what about that mysterious "red Hembarig," which Stanley Clisby Arthur identified in *Famous New Orleans Drinks* as "a popular sirup when old New Orleans was young"?

There's not a trace of a syrup called "hembarig" in the written record, whether in New Orleans or anywhere else. There are, however, abundant references to a syrup with a name that sounds quite similar: *himbeeressig*. This is simply the combination of the German words himbeer (raspberry) and essig (vinegar), and raspberry vinegar and sweetened raspberry vinegar syrup were indeed popular flavorings during the period. Arthur gathered many of his recipes by talking to old New Orleans bartenders, and it seems likely he was working phonetically and elided the spelling a bit when recording his Roffignac recipe.

Raspberry vinegar syrup was often called "raspberry shrub" in the nineteenth century (and still is by bartenders today), but that term appears to have been used primarily in New England and not in New Orleans. (A different form of shrub was a punch-like alcoholic beverage made by steeping fruit or fruit peels along with sugar in either brandy or rum.) Jerry Thomas's *How to Mix Drinks* (1862), America's first bartender's guide, includes a recipe for "Raspberry Shrub" that calls for steeping 3 quarts of raspberries in a quart of vinegar for a day, adding 8 pounds of sugar, and finishing the reduced mixture with 4 ounces of brandy for each pint of shrub. "Two spoonfuls of this," Thomas notes, "mixed with a tumbler of water, is an excellent drink in warm weather." Though he uses regular raspberry syrup in numerous recipes, Thomas does not incorporate raspberry vinegar shrub into any of his alcoholic drinks.

Christian Schultz's *Manual for the Manufacture of Cordials, Liquor, Fancy Syrups, & c.*, which was bound together with Thomas's bartender's guide as a single volume, includes three recipes for raspberry vinegar syrup. Each calls for various proportions of raspberries steeped in vinegar and boiled with sugar. There is also a recipe for raspberry shrub that consists of raspberry vinegar syrup fortified with a generous dose of good French brandy.

So Himbeeressig does indeed seem to have been, as Arthur claimed, "a popular sirup when old New Orleans was young"— though perhaps not under its German name. New Orleans grocers had been selling bottled raspberry vinegar alongside pickles, jellies, and preserves since at least the 1820s, and as soda fountains surged in popularity, the ingredient began to be used to flavor fizzy beverages, too. In 1868, Ernest Turpin, a wholesale confectioner who manufactured syrups alongside fancy candies, gum drops, and sugar almonds in his Old Levee Street shop, sent a sample of his raspberry vinegar to the *Daily Picayune* offices. In a note acknowledging the gift, the editors remarked, "This vinegar, with the addition of water, make a most palatable summer drink." Turpin regularly advertised his "superior syrups" to "those who keep Soda Saloons and Coffee-Houses." One such ad from 1869 includes raspberry vinegar alongside pineapple, lemon, orange flower, banana, rose, raspberry, strawberry, gooseberry, and vanilla as the flavors for his "French syrups for coffee houses."

New Orleans had a sizeable German-speaking population by this time, and some residents may well have called raspberry vinegar syrup *himbeeressig*. The term didn't make it into print locally, though, until the early twentieth cen-

FRENCH SYRUPS for COFFEEHOUSES

PAR EXCELLENCE.

100 dozen Pine Apple, Lemon, Orgeat, Orange Flower, Banana, Rose, Raspberry, Strawberry, Gooseberry, Vanilla and Raspberry Vinegar
These Syrups are manufactured expressly for family use under my personal supervision They are warranted pure and free from all adulteration. Great care has been taken to give to each quality the precise flavor of the fruit. To obtain this result pure juices have been imported direct from Europe. Call and examine, before purchasing elsewhere, at   ERNEST TURPIN'S.
                        93 Old Levee street,
Ja31—3t   between Conti and St. Louis.

Turpin advertisement for raspberry vinegar syrup, *Times-Picayune*, 1869.

tury. In 1906, the New Orleans Soda Water Company bobbled the spelling a bit when it listed "Himberr Essig" as the first of its six flavors of bar syrups, which it promised "are hard to beat." By the 1920s, two of the city's biggest restaurant supply houses, Loubat's Glassware & Cork Co. and J. E. Jung & Wolff Co., regularly included himbeeressig in their list of soda fountain syrups, though Jung & Wolff tended to spell it "himberg-essig."

Sharply tangy and also sweet, raspberry vinegar syrup would certainly add a nice zip to an ice-cold glass of soda water. Some pharmacists and soda water dealers started adding ingredients with even more kick to them, too. In 1861, a Cincinnati pharmacist named E. S. Wayne published an article entitled "Syrups" in *The Druggist* trade magazine. He opened by observing that "the season for the preparation and use of syrups for the soda fountain is at hand," then offered advice on economical methods for druggists to produce their own. "The addition of wines and spirits," Wayne noted, "with syrups of different flavors, has of late become quite common." The Cincinnati druggist did not condone such practices. "The propriety of pharmaceutists keeping such on their counters is very question-able," he concluded, "and should meet with no encourage-ment at their hands." The pharmacists of New Orleans saw things differently, and it was from the union of soda foun-tain syrup and hard liquor that the Roffignac was born.

CONFECTIONERS

As the Civil War neared, soda fountains could increasingly be found not only in druggist or soda water shops but also in New Orleans's flourishing confectionery stores. The increased availability and affordability of the same two in-gredients that helped drive the soda water trade—ice and sugar—also caused a boom in confectionery.

Most of the city's confectioners operated retail shops, where they made and sold a range of sweet treats for cus-tomers to purchase and either take home or eat on the premises. Their products included sugar-based creations like candies and pastries as well as frozen confections like ice cream and sherbets. The range of a typical New Orleans confectioner can be seen in an 1851 advertisement for an auction selling the entire stock of a retiring confectioner. The inventory consisted of "a large and well assorted lot of candies, preserves, cordials, glass jars and cases, dishes and stands, soda fountains and fixtures complete, marble-top stands, lamps, syrup bottles, toys, etc." The city's confectioners did a particularly brisk trade at Christmas, when families loaded up on sugar plums, French candied fruits, and chocolates, as well as decorated cornucopia and "fancy boxes"—painted paper or ornately carved wooden boxes—in which to put gifts.

The industry got a further boost in 1848, when a wave of revolutions swept through Europe. Many of the artisans who once served the great houses of European nobles—musicians, cooks, artists, and confectioners—found themselves out of work, and many sought better opportunities in the growing United States. In the years that followed, one new confectioner shop after another opened in New Orleans. These included the St. Charles Street shop of M. Lefort, who styled himself, "The King of Confectioners, late from Paris." In addition to pastries, cakes, and candies, he promised "the best collection of Flower Pictures, Statues, Fancy Goods, Fruits, Toys, etc. in pure sugar, which have ever before been seen in this city." In 1857, "M. Manry, Confectioner, direct from Paris" advertised that he had just opened a store on St. Anne Street, where he sold top-quality bonbons, chocolate-a-la-creme, sirup de Plesis aux Juis de Fruits, and "the finest Reine Claude Confitures [plum jams], direct from Paris."

The 1846 city directory listed just four confectioners along with two cake shops and three chocolate makers.

Advertisement for M. Lefort, King of Confectioners, *New Orleans Crescent*, 1850.

By 1861, the directory listed a total of fifty-eight confectioners, plus a half dozen cake bakers and four chocolate manufactures. Early confectionery shops had been scattered around the city, but by the eve of the Civil War they became increasingly concentrated along Canal Street. Since the 1840s, the city's higher end retailers of dry goods, clothing, and jewelry had been migrating from Chartres and Royal streets into newly constructed buildings on Canal Street, which were much larger than the older French Quarter shops. By the time the Civil War arrived, Canal Street had been transformed into a commercial center as well as a bustling entertainment district. Families out shopping and young couples seeking amusement were a prime market for candies, pastries, and refreshing beverages, and more and more confectioners were drawn to Canal Street to serve them.

Commerce came to a sudden halt during the Civil War, but New Orleans fell to Union troops with minimal fighting in April 1862. As a result, the city was spared the physical destruction that befell Charleston, Richmond, and Atlanta in the later years of the war. The retailers and confectioners on Canal Street struggled amid commercial disruptions and wartime inflation, but by 1864 business had begun to revive, and traffic surged after the war ended in 1865.

The career of Daniel Lopez, New Orleans's foremost confectioner in this period, reflects the larger trends in the city's commercial and social life. A native of Bordeaux, Lopez emigrated to the United States around 1848 and, in the early 1850s, established one of New Orleans's first chocolate manufactories in a small shop on Chartres Street. For a decade Lopez flourished in the French Quarter, but during the war years he found his customers increasingly drifting away to the trendy new blocks on Canal Street. His Christmas advertisements in 1863 sounded an almost desperate note. "Mr. Lopez," they read, "respectfully begs the public not to forget his house, although not situated on Canal Street." The following year he conceded to the inevitable and announced in October the grand opening of D. Lopez Ice Cream Saloon and Lunch for Ladies at the corner of Canal and Dauphine streets. His offerings included confectionery, sweet meats, ice creams, biscuits, and cordials. He soon engaged an Italian as his Chief Ice Cream Maker, and his ads promised "wines and liquors of all qualities," too.

It was along the bustling sidewalks of Canal Street in shops like Lopez's that the Roffignac was born.

CHAPTER THREE

AT LONG LAST, THE ROFFIGNAC APPEARS!

After Joseph Roffignac left New Orleans in 1828, his name lived on in the city primarily because of Roffignac Street. A short, eight-block stretch in what was then the suburb of St. Mary, it ran from the river levee westward to Camp Street, where its named changed to Terpsichore Street. Just after the Civil War, however, the name "Roffignac" began to appear in newspapers and public records in a rather different context.

On October 1, 1865, in its regular "Town Talk" column, the *New-Orleans Times* offered a sarcastic but intriguing commentary on soda fountains. "Town Talk is very fond of soda," it begins. "It is the temperance man's 'big drink.' The great solace to reformed 'tipplers,' for they can imbibe to their heart's content." There was a downside, though. Since soda water lacks any stimulants, reformed drinkers must "go through the motions of 'imbibing,' leaving to our imaginations to supply the desired stimulant. Unless, perchance, one more knowing than the rest, should accidentally hit on the right syrup."

The inventor of that new syrup, the author declares, was "a genius, a man of taste, and should be immortalized. . . . And Town Talk predicts that the name of Ruf. N. Yac will be honored by all temperance men for ages to come." Tongue planted firmly in cheek, Town Talk insists, "We never frequent bar-rooms. We never patronize 'tippling houses.' . . . When thirsty, we simply apply to the 'fountain of all good things'—Lopez—and call for a glass of *soda*."

The Lopez here is Daniel Lopez, the chocolatier and operator of the popular confectionery at the corner Canal and Dauphine streets. When it came to choosing a flavoring syrup, Town Talk professes to have "no part-'tickler' choice" but does observe that one syrup stood out because it cost three times more than the rest. "Many who indulge in this delectable 'syrup' seem somehow affected by—*the price!* and get very 'high up' occasionally." Some customers, furthermore, were so fond of the new syrup that they required very little soda water in it.

Here, as best as I can determine, is the first trace of a beverage called a Roffignac in New Orleans. It's not a cocktail but a specific kind of flavoring syrup, and it was found not in a bar-room or coffeehouse but at a confectioner's soda fountain.

Three years later, Roffignac syrup surfaced again, this time with a more standard spelling in the advertisements of a soda water dealer named Hugh McCloskey. A native of County Londonderry in Ireland, McCloskey had been in the fizzy water trade in New Orleans since the 1850s. His stand on the ground floor of Masonic Hall on St. Charles Street had long been one of the most well known in the city—so popular, in fact, that local newspapers took to calling him "Soda McCloskey." In 1868, he decided to follow the lead of Daniel Lopez and other competitors and set up shop on Canal Street. In May, McCloskey announced he was opening "a splendid saloon" near the corner of Canal and Chartres streets, complete with counters veneered in Louisiana cypress. "The price of my soda water and mead," he declared, "will be ten cents a glass (large glasses)"—the same as at his stand on St. Charles.

This grand opening announcement closed with a cryptic statement: "I sell no alcoholic beverages under the name Roffignac syrup, or other disguise." One wonders why the soda dealer felt compelled to devote a third of his three-sentence advertisement to such a denial. Was he sincerely distinguishing himself from other soda stands by refusing to sell booze? Or was he protesting with a wink and a nod so that his customers would know exactly what to ask for at his new shop?

It's impossible to know for sure. McCloskey offered similar denials in subsequent advertisements, though without referring to the name Roffignac. He noted in September 1869, for instance, "The public are reminded that no spirituous liquors are retailed at any of my establishments." He certainly was promoting his business as a place for family-friendly amusement. In 1870, the *Daily Picayune* declared that "McCloskey's soda water saloon" was "one of the most popular resorts of the public," noting its ice creams, cakes, and pastries served with delicious mead and "cool, sparkling soda bubbling out of silver fountains." Recently, the paper reported, McCloskey had enlarged his establishment "to the better accommodation of ladies and families."

Neither the Town Talk column nor McCloskey's ads provide much insight into the nature of this mysterious Roffignac syrup, though we can surmise that it contained a strong dose of alcohol and could be found at many of the confectioneries and soda fountains along Canal Street. Since Lopez's soda fountain is mentioned by name in the Town Talk's "Ruf. N. Yac" column, it's possible but not certain that he was the inventor of the formula.

More details emerged five years later. In July of 1873, New Orleans was gripped by a heat wave, with temperatures reaching 97 degrees Fahrenheit. To aid "his fellow sufferers," an intrepid reporter for the *Daily Picayune* hit the streets one sweltering evening and visited "the most fashionable drinking saloons" to learn "the mysterious art of concocting those mixtures so much demanded during this heated term." He sampled sherry cobblers, mint juleps, and "a new aspirant" called the Dolly Varden, named for a character in Charles Dickens's novel *Barnaby Rudge*. This last concoction started with a base of sugar, water, lemon juice, and a dash of raspberry syrup to which was added a generous slug of whiskey. The glass was then topped off with ice and garnished with assorted fruits, like pineapple, grapes, and strawberries.

The cobblers, juleps, and Dolly Vardens were saloon drinks, but the reporter found another popular cooling beverage in a different type of establishment. "As a kind of compromise," he noted, "the confectioneries make a deceptive beverage called 'Roffignac,' which for its powers for tangling feet is unexcelled. Whisky syrup and soda is the delusion."

The Roffignac, it seems, was made with whiskey from the start, not with cognac. It was meant from the outset to be a deceptive drink—hard liquor masked by syrup and soda. Unlike the Sazerac or the Ramos Gin Fizz, it wasn't associated with saloons or coffeehouses but rather with soda shops, pharmacies, and any other retailer who might have a soda fountain. Notably, none of these early references to the Roffignac mentions raspberries—although the trendy Dolly Varden, we should note, did include a dash of raspberry syrup along with the whiskey. Equally mysterious is the origin of the name. Was there some sort of connection, however tenuous, to the former mayor? Or was it just a name that had been lingering around town and sounded appealing? The historical record offers no clues.

What we do know is that here, in its earliest incarnation, Roffignac was clearly a specific type of soda fountain syrup. In August 1874, a series of newspaper ads urged newcomers who were looking for the best soda in New Orleans to head to "Harrison's, corner Magazine and Thalia street. He makes the syrups himself. You will find his nectar rich, creamy, and delicious. His chocolate, coffee, Roufignac, and all the fruit syrups are splendid." The druggist in question was William C. Harrison, who had been operating a pharmacy since at least 1866, and his use of Roffignac syrup would soon get him into hot water.

THE WAR AGAINST THE ROFFIGNACS

During the Civil War, President Lincoln signed into law the Revenue Act of 1862 to help fund the war effort. Along with an excise tax on whiskey and the nation's first income tax, the measure imposed annual license fees on a range of professions, including bankers ($100), jugglers ($20), tobacco dealers ($10), lawyers ($10), and peddlers (between $5 and $20, depending upon how many horses they traveled with). More germane to our purposes, those fees included a $20 annual license for all "retail dealers in liquors, including distilled spirits, fermented liquors, and wines of every description."

After the Civil War ended, the income tax and many of the license fees were repealed, but the cost of a retail liquor license was raised to $25. Until 1913, when the income tax was reinstituted, those excise and license taxes provided about 90 percent of all Federal revenue, and the government became increasingly determined to collect every dollar they could. In July 1877, Internal Revenue officials in New Orleans began cracking down on retail whiskey dealers and tobacconists who had not paid for a license. The following month they turned their sights on "the drug store men," as the *Daily Democrat* phrased it, "who, in order to turn an honest penny, dispense to their customers 'roffignacs' as a beverage during this warm spell."

The first "drug store man" to be charged was none other than William C. Harrison, who had boasted in his advertisements of the superiority of his own "Roufignac" syrup. Harrison was served a warrant at his stand at the corner of Magazine and Thalia streets and ordered to appear before U.S. Commissioner John P. Southworth. In a story headlined "A Raid on the Roffignacs," the *Daily Picayune* explained that the question before the court was "whether the sale of the drink called Roffignac by a druggist is retailing liquor under the statute of the United States." The prosecutors produced evidence that the Roffignac was composed of "syrup, plain soda and a small quantity, say a teaspoonful, of spirits to flavor it."

Harrison argued in his defense that a retail dealer of liquor was "one that sells liquor at a coffee-house or saloon, a soda fountain not being within the meaning of the statute." Furthermore, he asserted, Roffignac syrup did not infringe the revenue law because "a roffignac was merely a soda syrup flavored with spirits, as other syrups were flavored with vanilla, strawberry, etc." Notably, Harrison doesn't mention raspberry in his description, which leaves open the possibility that the syrup was meant to impart the flavor of whiskey to the drink. The *Picayune*'s prior characterization of the Roffignac as "deceptive," though, suggests that the flavor of the whiskey would have been masked somehow. If the beverage indeed had unexcelled "powers for tangling feet," it seems unlikely that the typical version contained only a teaspoonful of spirits—at least not for customers who signaled that they wanted theirs a tad stronger.

While Southworth was mulling over the initial test case, the *Picayune*'s reporter observed, "There is no use in winking at an apothecary until the Roffignac question is settled." Just one day later, the newspaper announced that the question had been "Settled in the Easiest Way." A druggist named Wadislaus L. Jurgieleweis, who also operated a shop on Magazine Street but had not been charged for a license violation, appeared before Commissioner Southworth and voluntarily purchased a $25 liquor license. That precedent set, William C. Harrison decided to throw in the towel, pay his fine, and buy a liquor license, too.

The relationship between alcohol and confectioners was further codified in 1882, when the Supreme Court of Louisiana ruled in favor of the city in *New Orleans vs. J Jané*. Jané had paid the required $25 confectioner license for his Canal Street shop but refused to purchase a separate liquor license, arguing that it was "part of the business of confectioneries, as conducted in New Orleans, to sell absinthe, vermouth and other liquors." The Supreme Court disagreed. The opinion noted "the prevalence of a custom in this City, among confectioners" to combine their businesses with that of "a barroom or drinking saloon," but concluded that custom simply "combines two kinds of business." Under the terms of the statute, a retailer conducting the two businesses together "is liable for a separate license on each."

FROM OUTLAW TO
LOCAL CLASSIC

The Roffignac's sneaky secret was finally out in the open, at least as far as the authorities were concerned. But it remained a drink of subterfuge for many New Orleanians. In 1885, the *Times-Democrat* commented on the enduring popularity of the "Ruffignac," noting that it was "considered delicate enough and of sufficiently respectable origin to be called for and drunk with propriety by ladies." As a result, the city's soda fountain men had "encouraged a popular delusion that it contains no alcohol, for which it is generally understood the ladies feel much gratitude."

Up to this point, it's worth noting, the Roffignac was associated primarily with confectioneries and soda fountains—establishments that were acceptable for women to patronize—and not with the male-only spaces of barrooms and coffeehouses. I've been able to turn up only a single example of a Roffignac being served in a barroom in the nineteenth century. It happened, not along Canal Street, but a mile further downtown in the Marigny, and the Roffignac in question—or, more accurately, the four Roffignacs—were served to a woman.

Around 7:00 p.m. on Friday, August 8, 1879, William Clark, an off-duty police officer, and one Mrs. Reilley entered Charles Green's oyster saloon on Decatur Street, just a half block off Elysian Fields. Both were already intoxicated, and they took seats in one of the private stalls in the back of the saloon and ordered more drinks. Clark, the *Times-Picayune* reported, "took four whisky straights and the woman four Ruffignacs." The two soon started arguing loudly, and suddenly a pistol shot rang out. As saloonkeeper Green cautiously approached the stall, Clark strode past him and out of the saloon. Green found Mrs. Reilley in the stall with her head slumped on the table, bleeding from a bullet wound just above her left ear. The police arrived soon after and put Mrs. Reilley in a cab to take her to the Charity Hospital, but she died en route. Clark was later arrested and sentenced to two years for manslaughter.

The Mrs. Reilley in this case was 27-year-old Celestine Fannie Reilley, née Le Blanc, a native of Iberville parish. She had been married at a young age to a man named Parker, who abandoned her. She then married James Reilley, with whom she had two children. A few months before her murder, the *Daily City Item* reported, Mrs. Reilley "took to drink," left her husband, and began "an intimacy" with Patrolman Clark, who himself was married and had two children. Newspaper accounts of the murder refer to Green's establishment as the "Dixie Oyster Saloon," the "Dixie Saloon," and simply a "drinking saloon." Regardless of the exact nature of the establishment, such a venue wasn't the type of place a respectable lady would want to be seen in the 1870s.

This scandalous incident aside, it seems that most New Orleans drinkers enjoyed their Roffignacs not in a saloon or hotel bar but at a confectionery or soda-water shop. The drink doesn't appear to have traveled very far outside of New Orleans, either. In 1880, Jules Guerre, a French immigrant who operated a confectionery in Shreveport, advertised that the soda water from his fountain was "as cold as if it was prepared in the Arctic region" and was served "with syrups or in roufignac, as pure as can be prepared." Further up the Mississippi in Natchez, F. Mannocci of the Marsh House advertised that he was serving "beverages of the season," which included plain and mixed drinks, lager beer, and "Roffignacs" for ten cents apiece. That, it seems, is as far as the beverage made it from its birthplace.

AN ASIDE ON COGNAC AND WHISKEY

There is considerable disagreement among cocktail enthusiasts today over the proper base spirit for a Roffignac. Some insist on using fine cognac brandy, arguing that that is what would have been in vogue at the time the Roffignac originated. Others prefer to use whiskey, either rye or bourbon, and those of a more compromising bent use a blend of cognac and whiskey. Nailing down which was the original spirit is complicated by the chronology of the Roffignac, for during the period in which it emerged drinkers in New Orleans were transitioning in their preferences from imported French brandy—especially brandy from the Cognac region—to domestically produced whiskey.

In the early 1870s, a fiendish, aphidlike bug called phylloxera spread through France's vineyards. By 1872, the cognac-producing Charente region was declared officially infected, and dry summers in 1873 and 1875 accelerated the bug's spread. Production of new brandy in and around Cognac plummeted from 225 million gallons in 1875 to just 17 million two years later. To conserve their inventories, producers began raising prices and limiting releases, since there was little new brandy to replenish their stocks. The rising prices, in turn, prompted a wave of disreputable operators to concoct imitation cognac from things like blended grain and beet spirits flavored with a splash of actual brandy and plenty of additives to simulate the flavor and color of the real thing. By the early 1880s, American newspapers declared that almost all French brandy being brought into the country was actually falsified and adulterated. American tipplers rapidly shifted to domestic whiskey, which had been steadily improving in quality, thanks to advances in distilling technology and the new practice of aging in charred oak barrels. American whiskey was on the rise, and the good name of Cognac was ruined for almost a century.

It was during this period that many of New Orleans's most popular cocktails, like Mint Juleps and Old Fashioneds, began to be made with whiskey. Perhaps the most famous transition is that of the Sazerac cocktail, whose name derives from an expensive brand of imported cognac brandy, Sazerac de Forge et Fils. How that name became affixed to a cocktail is a matter of some debate, but many note that "cocktail" was originally the name of a specific preparation made with sugar, water, and bitters. (The May 13, 1806, issue of the *Balance and Columbian Repository,* a Hudson, New York, newspaper, identified "Cock-tail" as "a stimulating liquor, composed of spirits of any kind, sugar, water, and bitters.") Brandy was one of the spirits commonly used, and if a customer wanted a particular brand of cognac, they may well have asked for "a

Sazerac cocktail." By the late nineteenth century, though, the Sazerac cocktail sold at the famous Sazerac House was made with rye whiskey.

In the twenty-first century, historically minded bartenders have started making many of the old classics with cognac instead of whiskey. Anyone attempting to recreate the Roffignac will have to decide how to account for that shift, but we should note that no description of the Roffignac from the nineteenth century mentions cognac. They all portray it as being a sneaky drink made with whiskey.

TEMPERANCE REVIVES

Virtually nothing has been written about the temperance movement in New Orleans, and for good reason. The anti-alcohol crusaders who were so effective elsewhere found little success in the Crescent City. In other parts of the South, including in the northern parishes of Louisiana, Methodists and Baptists were the primary drivers of temperance efforts. With its heavily Catholic population, the southern parishes, and especially New Orleans, were much slower to embrace the cause.

Before the Civil War, the South had lagged behind the rest of the United States in temperance organizing, and Louisiana had lagged far behind the rest of the South. In 1852, a visitor to New Orleans wrote to his son back in Maine, "The temperate societyes are striving hard to get a footing and a hearing here, but the place is so habituated to drunkenness that their task is a hard one." Temperance sentiment in the South went fallow amid the sectionalist tensions that led to the Civil War, but it began to revive during Reconstruction. Southern states, in fact, moved quickly to the head of the procession marching toward eventual nationwide prohibition. They were among the first to pass so-called "local option" laws, where individual counties and municipalities could vote to ban alcohol, and states like Georgia and Tennessee instituted statewide prohibition several years before the rest of the country.

The anti-saloon forces found less success in Louisiana, where the southern part of the state remained stubbornly wet, but this isn't to say the reformers didn't try. Temperance efforts in New Orleans tended to be more about using moral suasion to encourage people not to drink than attempting to outlaw alcohol. The New Orleans chapter of the Women's Christian Temperance Union (WCTU) was organized on March 2, 1876, with the stated objective "to inculcate temperance principles in the minds and hearts of the young" and "to use all Christian means and influences to induce reformation from the use of intoxicating drink." At the outset, the chapter's president later recalled, "The cause was unpopular and met with little encouragement."

The WCTU held regular meetings at the Young Men's Christian Association (YMCA) on Camp Street, as did the Sons of Temperance, which encouraged young men to sign a pledge of "T-Total" abstinence from alcohol. In the winter of 1879, the WCTU staged a series of gospel temperance meetings, and a committee of ladies visited all the Protestant ministers in the city (the Catholic priests, we can assume, were considered a lost cause) to encourage them to hold temperance-themed services and convince attendees to sign the teetotaler pledge.

Meanwhile, reformers were making more progress in other parts of the state. "For two years past," the *New-Orleans Times-Democrat* reported in 1884, "quite a temperance wave has been sweeping through Northern and Central Louisiana." More than twenty measures restricting alcohol in various ways, such as banning liquor sales near a school or church, had been put before the popular vote, and most had been successful. In 1886, the state legislature passed the so-called Sunday Law, "an act requiring all stores, shops, groceries, saloons, and all places of public amusement . . . to be closed on Sundays." Nominally, the measure was meant to enforce Sunday as a day of rest and forbid all but the most essential forms of commerce. In practice, those targeted for enforcement actions were mostly saloons and grocery stores that sold alcohol on Sunday.

In New Orleans, the Sunday Law was unpopular and widely flouted. The city's mayors and police chiefs wavered over the years between cursory enforcement and complete disregard, though every few years would see a flurry of prosecutions when a governor or dry-leaning newspaper put pressure on local authorities. The temperance forces faced an uphill battle in New Orleans, but they were successful in persuading many respectable citizens to avoid being seen drinking alcohol in public. Some of these respectable citizens found the Roffignac's deceptive nature to be quite useful for keeping up appearances.

In the early 1890s, the *Picayune* published a humorous essay musing on different types of eyes, including those of the "winking man," who inadvertently offends young women on the streets and buys unwanted items at auctions. "He may be a good deacon, in favor of Sunday laws," the writer quips, "yet the winking man will be humiliated in a drug store by his immoral wink, which will bring him Roffignac instead of plain soda."

In July 1892, *The Mascot*, a rather scandalous weekly illustrated newspaper, published an anti-temperance tale entitled, "He Fooled His Father." It opens by nodding at Methodist ministers and others "whose positions or circumstances preclude their taking such an open and honest course" as walking into a barroom and ordering a drink.

The author declares "taking the pledge" to be foolish, since "the man who cannot of his own volition abstain from liquor will not find the struggle against intemperance made easier by taking an oath of abstinence."

As an example, the author relates the story of a young man who had "cultivated the liquor habit so ardently and successfully that he took a jag to bed with him nearly every night." His father, a prominent cotton broker, and his mother begged him to amend his ways, and finally the young man broke down and agreed to go on the wagon. The father took his "jag haunted son" to the YMCA, where he signed the temperance pledge. The two then headed over to Canal Street and passed by McCloskey's soda fountain, where the father decided to "complete the day's good work" by introducing his now-reformed son to "the pleasure of soda water." The old man ordered a raspberry soda, and the son, who by this point had developed "a tremendous longing for a drink," solemnly ordered a Roffignac.

The Mascot author described the son's drink as "a soda water beverage, the base of which is whiskey and syrup." The father, however, was clueless as to its true nature. The son insisted on treating his father to a second round, and the older man ordered another raspberry soda and the younger another Roffignac. As they continued on down Canal Street, the son convinced his father to stop off for yet another soda water, and the son knocked back two more Roffignacs. "Coming upon top of his overnight debauch," the author relates, "those roufignacs revived the jag." The son fell sound asleep on the streetcar on the way home. The mystified father carried him to bed, then declared to his wife, "It's no use trying to cure the boy; he took the pledge then got drunk on sodawater."

CHAPTER FOUR

THE ROFFIGNAC IN THE TWENTIETH CENTURY

As the nineteenth century waned and the twentieth approached, the Roffignac transitioned from a sly soda water subterfuge to one of New Orleans's signature beverages— if not as an outright cocktail then at least as a distinctive alcoholic treat that visitors should try. In 1899 *The Harlequin*, a local weekly magazine, published a guide for tourists that instructed, "Before leaving French-town do not forget to treat your male friend to a roffignac at Mannessier's (he will find the name and the drink a novelty), and to an absinthe at the Old Absinthe House on Bourbon and Bienville."

Not every visitor was won over by the Roffignac. Roswell Field, Jr., a reporter for the *Chicago Evening Post,* visited New Orleans during Carnival in 1903 and filed a dispatch on "New Orleans Beverages." He praised the Sazerac, the "sirenlike" gin fizz, the mint julep, and the absinthe anisette but declared "the roufignac" to be "the first and only distinct disappointment. It seems to be merely an old-fashioned whiskey toddy, with about 60 per cent. of a sickening syrup." Field does not mention where he tried the Roffignac, but one wonders whether it was at a saloon along with more traditional cocktails or in its native habitat of a soda fountain or confectionery. Straight through until Prohibition, those businesses remained the most likely place to find a Roffignac, and a few such establishments developed quite a reputation for their versions.

The Mannessier's cited in the *Harlequin*'s guide was one of the city's longest-running and most popular confectioneries. Its founder, Auguste Mannessier, emigrated from France to New Orleans around 1848, and by 1861 he

Interior photograph of Mannessier's Confectionery. Courtesy Historic New Orleans Collection, 1974.25.27.391.

had opened a confectionery at 179 Canal Street. A decade later, he moved the business to Royal Street in the French Quarter, where he quickly became the city's premier ice cream-maker. (The *Times-Picayune* dubbed him "the renowned ice cream Mannessier" in 1872.) Every summer, a fleet of Mannessier's wagons, branded with distinctive blue-painted lanterns, were dispatched around the city to sell frozen treats along the streets.

It's a safe bet that Auguste Mannessier was serving Roffignacs alongside his ice cream by the time of the War on the Roffignacs. As early as 1866 he was advertising that "his cellars are provided with the best wines," and after moving the shop to Royal Street he touted Roman Punch and Champagne Punch as featured beverages. Mannessier passed away in 1880 at the age of 62, and his business was continued by his stepson Adolph S. Leclerc, who expanded the confectionery on Royal Street and operated it until he died in 1912. It was under Leclerc's ownership in the 1890s that Mannessier's began running weekly ads in *The Harlequin* and other local publications touting "The Mannessier Roffignac, associated with the fame of New Orleans for half a century," which might have been stretching the timeline just a bit.

Another popular destination for Roffignacs was the confectionery of Jules Domecq. Also French-born, he arrived in New Orleans in 1866 at the age of 20. He learned the ropes working as a pastry chef at well-known confectioneries like that of Desbons & Bonnecaze on St. Peter Street, and in 1875 he opened his own shop at the corner of Canal and Rampart. He moved up and down Canal Street several times over the next two decades, expanding the size and scope of his business in the process. In 1885, Domecq went into a partnership with one Alexander Grouchy and bought out the confectionery of his old boss, Edward Bonnecaze, at the corner of Canal and Baronne. The splendidly named Grouchy & Domecq operated their "Ladies' and Gents' Lunch Restaurant and Ice Cream Saloon" until it was destroyed by fire in 1890. Domecq took that opportunity to strike out on his own again and move into a newly erected building on Canal between Bourbon and Dauphine streets.

Now proclaiming himself "Jules Domecq, Confectioner and Restaurateur!," he touted first and foremost his pastries, candies, and bonbons. Domecq made no pretense of running a dry establishment though. His "Lunch Saloon for Ladies and Gentlemen as well as a restaurant" would dispense choice wines . . . at moderate prices." He also promoted "a bar where the finest liquors will be kept," including "Whiskies, Cognac, Liquors from the celebrated house of Leon Lamothe."

The ambiguous nature of the Roffignac—a beverage somewhere between a soft drink and a hard cocktail, between respectability and scandal—continued to create legal troubles for those who served them. In February 1901, Jules Domecq was arrested for violating the Sunday Law. The action outraged the wet-leaning *Times-Democrat*, which explained, "Domecq does not run a barroom but a confectionery and restaurant. There is a tradition, however, that if a customer at the soda water counter calls for a roffignac . . . he will not be compelled to leave the place thirsty." The newspaper expressed surprise that "this comparatively inoffensive establishment for the accommodation of jags" would be singled out for Sunday law enforcement considering there were twenty or more establishments in the same vicinity that could be brought up on the same charges.

Jules Domecq was surprised and outraged himself, and he told the newspapers he suspected he was the victim of "a dirty trick" and that his arrest must have been ordered "on the complaint of a private enemy." When the confectioner appeared before the Second City Criminal Court the following week, the two arresting detectives testified that they had received special orders from the chief of police to watch Domecq's confectionery. The judge also found it odd that Domecq was the only one arrested that Sunday for violating the liquor laws. He declined to arraign the confectioner, saying he would take the case under advisement "until such a time as the police see fit to enforce the law without discrimination."

SPINNING TALES

As the Roffignac began to be regarded as a signature New Orleans drink, various writers sought to explain how the curiously named cocktail came to be. They tended to start with the name itself, and most drew a direct link to the old mayor. Perhaps the first was the French Creole historian Charles Gayarré, who in 1887 published a sketch in *American Magazine* entitled, "A Street in Old New Orleans." It includes the tale of Mayor Roffignac (whose name Gayarré spells Rouffignac) and an infamous New Year's Day "Firecracker Battle."

It all began when a firecracker skirmish among a few boys was joined by a group of young men and eventually swelled to a riotous crowd battling from Bourbon to Royal streets. As nightfall approached, Mayor Roffignac attempted to restore order by dispatching fifty members of the City Guard armed with bayonets, with Roffignac himself marching at the head of the formation. The sight of bayonets only inflamed the crowd, Gayarré writes, and "the municipal guard retreated to their quarters under a prodigious shower of explosive blank cartridges."

Roffignac, undaunted, turned to face the mob and demanded solemnly, "Gentleman, what means this disorderly conduct? Is it rebellion against the laws of the State, or is it my life you seek?" Baring his breast with a dramatic sweep of his hand, the mayor declared, "If my life, take it!"

The crowd responded by pelting Roffignac with "a score of well-directed firecrackers," which caused him to utter "a dismal shriek." The mob roared with laughter, and the riotous spell was broken. The people began shouting, "Hurrah for Roffignac, who has sacrificed himself and died for his country!"

"In commemoration of that mighty event," Gayarré concludes, "a barkeeper invented a drink which he called a 'Rouffignac,' and which to this day has remained as popular as the name of the worthy magistrate." Anyone wishing to learn more about the subject "has only to call at one of the fashionable soda-shops in Canal Street and ask for a Rouffignac." Gayarré provides no source for his tale. If an "infamous" firecracker battle indeed took place on New Year's Day in the 1820s, no trace of it remains in the surviving newspapers.

Subsequent writers not only linked the mayor with the beverage but credited Roffignac himself as the inventor. In *New Orleans as It Was* (1895), Henry C. Castellanos included a biographical sketch of Joseph Roffignac that ends with a short meditation on the ephemerality of fame. The once-beloved mayor, Castellanos observes, was a man of many talents and an intimate of some of the era's leading statesmen. "And yet in this day of grace and progress," he mused, "who mentions the name of Roffignac except at a soda water stand? He is known only as the inventor of a fashionable beverage. Such is fame!"

A few years later, James S. Zacharie made a similar claim in an address to the Louisiana Historical Society on the topic, "New Orleans—Its Old Streets and Places." Roffignac Street was no more, he explained, for it had been renamed Terpsichore back in the 1870s. Originally, though, it was named "in honor of a mayor of New Orleans, who is jovially known as the inventor of the drink of whisky and soda called after him."

Sidney Story added more color to the tale in an essay on "Famous New Orleans Drinks," which was included in a slim cocktail book called *Beverages De Luxe* (1914). Story highlights five distinctive Crescent City cocktails: the Sazerac, the Ramos Gin Fizz, Absinthe a la Suisse, the Peychaud Cocktail, and "High Ball Roffignac." On "the most fashionable block" of Canal Street, he explains, can be found "the well-known confectionery establishment of Harry Schaumburg. Here the gentlemen of leisure will saunter in to refresh themselves with a 'Roffignac High Ball,' which is exhilarating and delicious in taste and flavor." (Schaumburg, we should note, had purchased Jules Domecq's Canal Street confectionery and restaurant in 1903.)

Story, unfortunately, does not describe the delicious flavor of the Roffignac, so it's not clear whether raspberry-flavored syrup had yet entered the recipe. He does claim, however, that the cocktail was invented by Mayor Roffignac himself back "during the Ancien regime." Roffignac's office, he asserts, was routinely thronged each afternoon with "visitors desirous of both paying their respects to the Knightly Rofignac and also enjoying one or two of his delicious 'Rofignacs.'" Story's calling the drink a "high ball" suggests that it was becoming associated more with the world of cocktails than with soda fountain drinks. That term emerged in the 1890s, much later than the Roffignac itself, and it refers to a tall glass with a shot of whiskey and ice that is filled to the top with soda. Depending upon how much soda one uses, one could indeed classify the Roffignac as a high ball.

That's exactly how the *Donaldsonville Chief* characterized the drink in 1914 when it broke some remarkable news: the original recipe for the Roffignac, the "father of the American high-ball," had been found in New Orleans! The city, it seems, was preparing for the 100th anniversary of Andrew Jackson's victory at the Battle of New Orleans, and the recipe in question was found beneath an old floor in the Spanish armory. The newspaper account provides a wealth of detail about the Roffignac's origins. The French count, it seems, was a "well-known Creole bon vivant," and he concocted the drink sometime before 1815. When General Andrew Jackson arrived to plan the defenses of the city, "the Roffignac was all the rage at Maspero's, Tremoulet's, and the other exchanges and coffee houses." The future president, a devoted fan of Madeira, was convinced by one sip to change his allegiances to Roffignac's cocktail.

In a surprising turn, the *Chief* reveals that instead of a popular mayor creating the cocktail, it was the cocktail that made the mayor. "Roffignac's success in having a drink named after him," the *Chief* explained, "placed him at once in the public eye. In 1820 he was selected mayor and served several terms." Over time, though, the original recipe "gradually gave way to the regulation whiskey highball, which was patterned after it." When General Jackson visited the city again in 1828, he was disappointed to find he could not secure a Roffignac.

One would expect that a newspaper story about the discovery of the original Roffignac recipe would include the recipe itself. It's possible that the *Donaldsonville Chief*'s story did. Incredibly, all surviving versions of the November 7, 1914, issue were copied from the same original microfilm image, which has the ending of the Roffignac story obscured beneath a large black circle—apparently a damaged spot in the microfilm. I have tried to turn up a paper copy or non-damaged microfilm version of that issue but have so far been unsuccessful. I don't think it would reveal much of value, though, since the rest of the details in the story are clearly fabricated from whole cloth. It's safe to assume that the "original recipe," if it was indeed included, would have been the product of creative license, too.

Not every authority credited the mayor with inventing the Roffignac. When the famous Canal Street caterer and confectioner Jules Domecq died in 1921, at least three local newspapers declared him to be "the creator of the popular drink to which he gave the name 'ruffignac,'" as the *Times-Picayune* put it. That claim seems highly unlikely, since Domecq did not arrive in the United States until 1866, a year after the "Ruf. N. Yac" was recorded as being served at Daniel Lopez's confectionery.

PROHIBITION INTRUDES

On August 8th, 1918, Louisiana became the fourteenth state to ratify the 18th Amendment, with the "dry" forces in the legislature from the northern and central parishes edging out the "wet" votes of the southern parishes. Five months later, Nebraska became the thirty-sixth ratifying state, and at midnight on January 17, 1920, the entire United States went officially dry. The thirteen years that followed wreaked havoc on America's century-old cocktail tradition and its thriving restaurant culture, since most restaurants then, as now, depended on alcohol sales to make a profit. Prohibition almost killed off the Roffignac, too.

Between 1920 and 1933, the word Roffignac (and its variant spellings) all but disappear from the written record. The few newspaper stories in which the name is found are making historical references to the mayor, not his namesake beverage, with one notable exception. A feature by Helene Robbins in the October 10, 1926, issue of the *Times-Picayune* recounts the "Soft Drinks and Sweets of Our Grandparents." Surveying the history of soda fountain treats in New Orleans, Robbins cites the "glory of 'rouffignac' and mead," describing the former as "a more manly drink of the period and one known only to New Orleans" and "made of seltzer or soda water, rock syrup and Bourbon whiskey." (Again, no mention of raspberry.)

One might think that the Roffignac, considering its long history of hiding an alcoholic kick within sweet soda water, might have been the perfect tipple for the Prohibition era. Indeed, soda fountains and confectioneries flourished during the 1920s. "Soft Drinks, Retail"—a category that didn't exist in the 1919 New Orleans City Directory—blossomed to fill more than three full pages comprising over four hundred names in the 1920 edition. A little spot-checking shows that almost every one of these new "soft drink" retailers was listed the year before as operating a saloon.

Of course, the Roffignac's true alcoholic nature had long been exposed, so it's not surprising that businesses—be they confectioneries, soda fountains, or new "soft drink" retailers—would refrain from advertising that they were selling Roffignacs even if they did dispense a beverage that looked and tasted very similar. Once cocktails and hard liquor drinks of all sorts had to be served on the sly, the Roffignac seems to have lost its *raison d'être*. In New Orleans, as in the rest of America, drinking moved from the saloon into the speakeasy—or into the "blind tiger," as illegal saloons were more commonly called in the South. In the process, the decades-long taboos that had made the saloon a male-only environment rapidly dissolved.

The Roffignac seems to have faded quite quickly from local memory. In 1931, the *Times-Picayune* ran a story about a new project at City Hall to review, repair, and catalog old books and records from the city's archives. As an example of the many valuable finds, the archive keeper cites a volume dated 1823 that includes a handwritten message from Mayor Roffignac. "I am told that a famous cocktail was named after Roffignac," she comments. "It was known all over the world during that time. The recipe has since been lost."

RESURRECTING THE ROFFIGNAC

The recipe for the Roffignac had not in fact been lost, and it didn't take any rummaging beneath the floorboards of an old Spanish armory to rediscover it. Instead, it appeared within the pages of that slim, somewhat eccentric cocktail book published by Stanley Clisby Arthur in 1937.

Arthur was born in Merced, California, in 1881. He attended Stanford University, then embarked on a career as a newspaperman, working for papers in California and Texas before moving to New Orleans in 1907 to become a reporter and cartoonist for the *Item*. There he met Ella McMillan Bentley, herself an accomplished author and journalist.

Bentley's father founded the *Donaldsonville Chief,* and she served as that newspaper's associate editor for several years, before moving to New Orleans to contribute to the *Times-Democrat* and magazines like *Puck.* The two were married in 1908 and promptly headed east, where Stanley worked for newspapers in New York City and Ella wrote poetry and a well-received children's book entitled *Sonny Boy's Day at the Zoo.*

The Arthurs returned to New Orleans in 1913, and Stanley, a devoted outdoorsman, took the position of state ornithologist for the Louisiana Department of Conservation. He went on to become the director of the department's Wild Life Division, retiring in 1930 to devote his energies to writing. In his books, Arthur alternated between nature and history, with titles including *Fur Animals of Louisiana* (1931), *Stories of the West Florida Rebellion* (1934), *Old New Orleans: A History of the Vieux Carré* (1936), and *Audubon: An Intimate Life of the American Woodsman* (1937). It was in *Old New Orleans* that Arthur first wrote about the Roffignac cocktail. In his entry on "Mayor Roffignac's," a red brick building at 721 Royal Street purportedly erected by the mayor in the early nineteenth century, Arthur provides a capsule biography of Roffignac and notes that a drink was named in his honor. "To make a Roffignac?" he writes. "Certainly. Take whiskey three-fifths, syrup two-fifths (either red Hembarig, grenadine, or raspberry) and add seltzer or soda water . . . and that's all there was to a Roffignac."

Arthur expanded on that description the following year, when he wrote what would prove his best-selling and longest-lasting book: *Famous New Orleans Drinks & How to Mix 'Em*. A slim volume of just ninety-seven pages, it was published by J. S. W. Harmanson, a bookseller on Royal Street who published locally themed books on the side. Prohibition had ended just four years earlier, and Americans were still recovering a cocktail culture that had almost been lost. In his preface, Arthur hails New Orleans as "the home of civilized drinking," arguing that the mixing of drinks "has constituted as high an art in this Creole city as the incomparable cooking for which it is famed." His stated goal for the book is "to acquaint the world—or that part of the world that may be interested—with the art of mixing a drink as it is done in New Orleans."

Famous New Orleans Drinks and How to Mix 'Em dust jacket.

For sources, Arthur drew on material uncovered during his research for *Old New Orleans* and other historical books, but the recipes themselves were "cajoled from old and new experts." He was given the recipe for the Sazerac cocktail by Leon Dupont, who before Prohibition had been a cocktail mixer at Thomas Handy's Sazerac House. The formula for the Vieux Carré was provided by its originator, Walter Bergeron, head bartender at the Hotel Monteleone, while the proper ratio for a martini was offered by John Swago of the St. Regis Restaurant. (Remember the names Dupont and Swago—they'll pop back up in a minute.)

Many of Arthur's historical claims should be taken with a healthy dose of skepticism. He asserts, for instance, that the apothecary Antoine Amédée Peychaud, creator of New Orleans's famous brand of bright red bitters, also invented the drink known as the cocktail. The name, Arthur explains, came from Peychaud's serving the drink in a double-ended egg cup the French called a *coquetier,* which English-speaking New Orleanians soon corrupted to "cocktail." It is true that Peychaud created the bright red bitters that bear his name, but the rest is either Arthur's invention or a fable told by one of his "old and new experts." If anyone ever served mixed drinks in an egg cup in New Orleans, it wasn't recorded in any historical record. In 1806, when the *Balance and Columbian Repository* defined "cocktail" as "a stimulating liquor, composed of spirits of any kind, sugar, water, and bitters.," A. A. Peychaud would have been around three years old.

More egregious, Arthur silently excises inconvenient facts that don't support his narrative. He cites the discussion of cocktails in Henry Didimus's 1845 book *New Orleans As I Found It,* quoting Didimus's description of a brandy cocktail as having the same ingredients as a brandy toddy "with the addition of a shade of bitters." Didimus's original passage, however, reads: "with the addition of a shade of *Stoughton's* bitters." It seems unlikely that this elision was accidental, for Didimus's specifying Stoughton's bitters instead of Peychaud's in 1845 certainly undercuts the notion that Peychaud was the originator of the cocktail.

So we have to be a little bit cautious when we get to Arthur's treatment of the Roffignac, which he includes as the final entry in the book's "Whiskey Drinks" chapter. While he does not offer a specific date for the Roffignac's invention, he does term it "a favorite tipple of Old New Orleans" and notes that while "not so celebrated as A. A. Peychaud's cocktail, it was equally potent"—both of which suggest antebellum roots. That suggestion is reinforced by Arthur's description of the misnamed "red Hembarig" as "a popular sirup when old New Orleans was young." Many years later, this implied chronology would throw off quite a few cocktail history sleuths as they tried to follow Arthur's trail.

Arthur may have set out "to acquaint the world" with the art of New Orleans cocktails, but his book drew little notice outside of its home city. The *Times-Picayune* and Arthur's old employer, the *Daily Item,* both published cursory reviews, the latter concluding that the book "should prove a boon to the native who is necessarily expected to supply such necessary and important information to thirsty pilgrims from afar." As far as I can find, no newspaper outside of New Orleans published a review or even a brief notice of the book's publication. Arthur's volume proved to have staying power locally, though. It appeared regularly alongside other New Orleans–themed books in the ads for the Holmes department store on Canal Street, and it remained a staple in New Orleans gift shops for decades to come. By 1954 it was in its tenth printing.

Stanley Clisby Arthur passed away in 1963 at the age of 82. The following year, his son John told Howard Jacobs of the *Times-Picayune* that, of all his books, his father most enjoyed writing *Famous New Orleans Drinks* because "he found the research for the tome most invigorating." The book fell out of print briefly, but in 1965 John Arthur renewed the copyright, and the following year published the fourteenth printing of the slim volume. It has remained in print ever since.

ANOTHER QUICK ASIDE ON COGNAC

Readers in the 1930s who took Arthur's advice to "use cognac, as in the original drink" could actually make a Roffignac Roffignac if they so desired, for by that point there was an imported brandy on the American market named

Roffignac Cognac. Its origins have nothing to do with the cocktail with which it shares a name, but it does have at least a tenuous link to the former mayor of New Orleans. The brand was produced at Chateau Chesnel, an Italian-style castle built in 1610 near Cognac, in southwest France. The chateau was passed down through several generations of the Chesnel family and ended up, through various marriages, being owned by members the Roffignac family. Count Ferdinand de Roffignac inherited the chateau in the late 1800s and began distilling and aging brandy there. In 1923 he launched the brand Cognac Comte Ferdinand de Roffignac, which is still produced at the chateau today.

Ferdinand de Roffignac was the great-grandson of Charles-Philippe de Roffignac, Joseph Roffignac's youngest brother, so the cognac maker was the great-grandnephew of the New Orleans mayor. The company began exporting its brandies to the United States after Prohibition ended, and by the mid 1930s advertisements for it were appearing regularly in American newspapers and magazines, where it was often called, simply, "Roffignac Cognac." That brand has caused some commentators to speculate that the Roffignac cocktail may have been named after the spirit and not the mayor, but the cognac didn't appear on the scene until more than half a century after New Orleanians were sipping Roffignacs on Canal Street.

THE POST-PROHIBITION ROFFIGNAC

As New Orleans's drinking scene rebounded in the wake of Repeal, many of its most famous cocktails enjoyed a revival, too. Pete Cazebonne, who had operated the Old Absinthe House before Prohibition, took his old water-dripper and other bar fixtures out of storage and was once again serving Absinthe Frappés on Bourbon Street. The Sazerac Company, which owned the trademark to the famous cocktail, leased a storefront on Carondelet Street and created a replica of the old Sazerac Bar, complete with four bartenders who had worked at the original Royal Street location. Henry C. Ramos had closed his bar in 1919 and died in 1928, but his estate licensed the trademark and recipe for Ramos's signature cocktail to the Hotel Roosevelt, which declared its bars to be the home of "The Original and Only Ramos Gin Fizz."

It took a bit longer for the Roffignac to reemerge, and the first place it popped up was at the St. Regis Restaurant on Royal Street. The restaurant had been around since 1926, and Leon Dupont, who had been a bartender at Ramos's before Prohibition, was one of its founders. In 1934, the St. Regis brought on another Ramos alum, John Swago, as head bartender. The restaurant's advertisements in the mid-1930s focus on the food offerings, but a full-page ad in 1939 includes a list of "Bar Specials." Alongside the St. Regis Cocktail (15 cents) and the "Ginn Fizz, New Orleans Special" (20 cents) is an "Old Time Rouffignac" (also 20 cents). It was still on the menu a year later in 1940, though its price had risen to 30 cents.

Did Dupont or Swago, who provided Stanley C. Arthur with the Sazerac and Martini recipes for *Famous New Orleans Drinks,* also give him the Roffignac formula with the mysterious "red Hembarig" syrup? It's quite possible. The St. Regis's advertisements include a section at the bottom thanking their many suppliers. Perhaps not coincidentally, among them is the "Loubat Glassware & Cork Co.," which had been carrying Himbeer Essig as one of its soda fountain syrup flavors since at least the 1920s.

LAST CALL AT MAYLIE'S

The St. Regis closed in the 1950s, but the Roffignac lived on as the house cocktail in a rather unlikely spot: Maylie's Restaurant on Poydras Street, which at the time was one of the oldest restaurants in the city. The establishment dated back to 1878, when two French immigrants, Jean Bernard Maylie and his brother-in-law Hipolyte Esparbe, opened a saloon across the street from the Poydras Market, where Maylie had previously had a butcher stall. They catered at first to butchers from the market, who began their days as early as 3:00 a.m. By the time the butchers knocked off in the late morning and headed across the street to Maylie & Esparbe's bar, they were ravenously hungry. After much persuasion, Marie Jeanne Esparbe, Hipolyte's wife, began to prepare a 11:00 a.m. lunch, which proved a hit. Within a few years, Maylie and Esparbe added a small dining area beside the bar, and by the 1890s the restaurant was serving an evening dinner, too.

Straight through until Prohibition, Maylie & Esparbe operated as a self-declared "stag table d'hôte" restaurant, meaning it served men only and offered just two fixed-menu meals each day, lunch at 11:00 a.m. and dinner at 6:00 p.m. Maylie's, as the restaurant was popularly known, became famous for those dinners, for which customers purchased tickets in advance and sat together at long common tables. The meal always began with *bouilli* (a.k.a. "boiled soup meat")—a brisket or similar beef cut slow-simmered until tender and served with horseradish, ketchup, fresh French bread, and butter. The other courses varied each day—boiled crabs with cream gravy and rice on Fridays, spaghetti with tomato sauce on Monday—accompanied by crisp salads.

There is no evidence that Roffignacs were served at Maylie's before Prohibition. Early twentieth-century accounts of the stag dinners note that no liquor was served during the meal, only top-quality red wines. After a dessert of ginger snaps, cheese, and fruit, guests would retire to the long mahogany bar, where they received "coffee in thick glasses, with a thimbleful of cognac accompanying it."

J. B. Maylie died in 1907 and Hipolyte Esparbe in 1912, but the restaurant kept on, with Madame Esparbe running the kitchen and Maylie's two sons, John and William, managing everything else. Maylie's continued serving its famous stag lunches and dinners after Prohibition arrived, but the old bar on the corner, the *Times-Picayune* reported, was converted to "a soft drink establishment for workers in the market and their customers." Not all the drinks served at Maylie's were soft, however. In September 1926 federal agents raided the restaurant during a banquet being held for forty-five railroad men. They found five gallons of wine and a small quantity of liquor and arrested William Maylie for alcohol possession.

The Prohibition years brought other changes, too. Madame Esparbe died in 1923, but the cooks who had worked in her kitchen for years, most of them African American men, continued preparing the same repertoire of Creole-inflected dishes. In 1932, the city of New Orleans decided

Photo courtesy of WWL-TV

Roffignac
OLD
NEW ORLEANS
FAVORITE...

Here's how to make it:
Fill Old Fashioned glass with ice cubes. Pour in 1 oz. brandy or cognac, ½ oz. rye whisky, grenadine syrup to taste and a squirt of seltzer water. Twist piece of lemon peel over drink, stir and serve on rocks. If you prefer, prepare it with crushed ice in shaker, blend, strain and serve as a cocktail.

Carte de la Liquer Et Des Vins

ESTABLISHED 1876

RESTAURANT MAYLIE

1009 POYDRAS STREET
(near O'Keefe)

NEW ORLEANS, LA.

Maylie's Restaurant menu. Courtesy Historic New Orleans Collection, gift of Richard and Rima Collin, 93-404-RL.444.

that the Poydras Market, which had been declining in traffic for years, was no longer needed, and the sheds were torn down to make more street space for automobiles.

It's not clear when Maylie's started serving the Roffignac, but by the 1950s it had become the restaurant's signature cocktail. A menu from the 1960s not only includes the Roffignac in its "Suggestions from Our Antique Bar" ($1.00) but also features on its cover the recipe for "Roffignac: Old New Orleans Favorite." The instructions are simple: fill an Old Fashioned glass with ice cubes, pour in an ounce of brandy or cognac and a half ounce of rye whiskey, and finish with grenadine syrup to taste and a squirt of seltzer water.

With just a squirt of soda and served in an Old Fashioned glass, this certainly sounds like a cocktail and not a soda fountain drink, which makes identifying its lineage difficult. Did Maylie's introduce the Roffignac during Prohibition as part of its soda fountain offering—and perhaps with a dose of whiskey hidden sneakily inside? Or was it added after Prohibition, when the proprietors could once again (legally) serve more than just glasses of coffee across their brown wooden bar? If it were added later, did the Maylies consult Stanley Arthur's *Famous New Orleans Drinks & How to Mix 'Em* when settling on their recipe? It's possible. Arthur, after all, calls for a jigger (1.5 ounces) of whiskey or cognac in his version, and grenadine is one of the three options for the "sirup." Maylie's version follows that same basic formula.

By the time Maylie's Roffignac recipe appeared on its menu, the restaurant was in decline. In 1959 the widening of Dryades Street (since renamed O'Keefe Street) resulted in the city taking and demolishing the old brick building that housed Maylie's bar, leaving just the larger two-story frame building with the dining room and kitchen on the ground floor and the Maylie family's living quarters upstairs. One by one, the houses on surrounding blocks, which were once home to many of Maylie's patrons, were torn down and replaced by office buildings, the new City Hall and Civil Court, and eventually the Super Dome. The six-course table d'hôte dinner remained (costing $6.50 by 1974), with boiled beef brisket and potatoes still the anchoring course followed by Creole dishes like deviled eggs remoulade, turtle soup, gumbo, and bread pudding. By this point, business had dwindled so much that the two proprietors, William and Anna May Maylie, and a single waiter could handle the customers.

In 1986, the Maylies decided it was time to retire. They put the building up for sale, and on New Years Eve the restaurant served its last table d'hôte dinner. The Roffignac cocktail seemed destined to disappear along with it.

CHAPTER FIVE

RECREATING
THE ROFFIGNAC

In the first decade of the twenty-first century, the Roffignac was rescued from history's dust bin by the craft cocktail revival. Most reconstructors based their recipes on the one found in Arthur's *Famous New Orleans Drinks,* and they tended to use cognac for the base spirit. Unable to track down the elusive red Hembarig, they tried either raspberry syrup or grenadine. Few were impressed with the results.

In 2011, I published a series of blog posts that were, as far as I am aware, the first to identify that Arthur's mysterious ingredient was most likely *himbeeressig,* a.k.a. raspberry vinegar or raspberry shrub. Others picked up on that nugget and ran with it, and with raspberry shrub as its flavoring, the cocktail has experienced what might generously be termed a minor revival over the past decade.

I can't take credit for that part. Legendary New Orleans bartender Paul Gustings was perhaps the first in the city to incorporate raspberry shrub into the Roffignacs he served at Broussard's Empire Bar. In 2014 he provided his recipe to *Saveur,* and it calls for a hefty amount of shrub—2½ ounces—shaken with 1½ ounce cognac and ½ ounce simple syrup. That blend is strained into a tall, ice-filled glass and topped with soda water. Gustings, *Saveur* noted, opted for cognac instead of whiskey as "a nod to Roffignac's Gallic heritage."

Chris Hannah is another historically minded bartender who has helped drive the cocktail revival in New Orleans. He named The Jewel of the South, his bar and restaurant on St. Louis Street, after the antebellum coffeehouse of Joseph Santini, the inventor of the Brandy Crusta. The Roffignac at the Jewel of the South is almost ruddy brown

The Roffignac at the Jewel of the South. Photograph courtesy of the author.

in hue. Hannah starts not with a raspberry shrub but a fruit syrup to which he adds a little vinegar at mixing time to create a shrub *á la minute.* That, in turn, is mixed with cognac and served over ice cubes in a tall collins glass. A single blackberry on a bamboo pick and a paper straw speckled with tiny black fleurs-de-lis finish the glass.

The fruit syrup gives the drink a darker and richer character, more tart cherry than bright raspberry, but it's still quite crisp, and pretty boozy, too. Hannah told me that he came up with his version after he moved to New Orleans to be head bartender for Arnaud's French 75 bar, a position he held for fourteen years. While at the French 75, he began experimenting with old New Orleans classics that had fallen by the wayside, like Santini's Brandy Crusta. For the Roffignac, Hannah told me, "I started with the recipe on the menu from Maylie's."

The Roffignac has since popped up on other New Orleans bar menus, too. It's served today alongside caviar and fine champagne at the ornate Chandelier Bar in the lobby of the Four Seasons Hotel. The Chandelier version blends cognac with a raspberry-citrus shrub and seltzer, and it's served over ice in a fluted collins glass with a garnish of raspberries, lemon peel, and a spray of mint.

Back in 2014, the famed Carousel Bar at the Hotel Monteleone had a Roffignac in the "New Orleans Classics" section of its cocktail menu, made with Pierre Ferrand Ambre Cognac, raspberry syrup, and soda water. It was no longer on the menu when I visited in May of 2022, but I asked the bartender if he could mix one up anyway. After rummaging around in a cabinet and collecting a few bottles, he produced what could best be described as a raspberry-flavored cognac highball—fizzy and refreshing, if not particularly deep in flavor.

There's no New Orleans craft cocktail joint named "The Roffignac Bar" (at least not yet), but in the space of the decade the Roffignac has made a quiet comeback. When Philip Green itemized New Orleans's "all-star menu of cocktails" for the *Daily Beast* in 2019, he included the Roffignac in the middle of the list of eleven, right between La Louisianne and the Brandy Crusta.

PERMUTATIONS AND COMBINATIONS

On a warm Friday morning in May, Neal Bodenheimer unlocked the door and let me into Cure, his cocktail bar on Freret Street, for an impromptu Roffignac tasting session. Perhaps no one has been a more passionate advocate for the Roffignac than Bodenheimer. A New Orleans native, he opened Cure in 2009, then went on to launch three more restaurants and bars in the city, Cane & Table, Val's, and Peychaud's. In 2018, Cure won the James Beard Award for Outstanding Bar Program. Four years later, he and Emily Timberlake published *Cure: New Orleans Drinks and How to Mix 'Em,* which is a recipe book but also a guide to drinking and eating in the Crescent City. The photo on the cover is of a pristine orange-pink Roffignac in a tall-stemmed glass, bathed in sunlight on the corner of a marble-topped bar.

As my eyes adjusted to the dark interior at Cure, I spied a big Vitamix blender on the bar top, its clear container filed with yet-unmixed layers of white granulated sugar, white vinegar, and water. Bobbing at the top was a raft of bright red raspberries. Bodenheimer's shrub recipe is easy to remember: equal parts of all four ingredients. That day, it was two cups of each. As we chatted, Bodenheimer flipped on the Vitamix and let it whir, starting at low speed then punching it higher and higher. A minute later the contents had been transformed into a thick puree with the same bright pink hue as Pepto-Bismol. He poured that mixture into a wire mesh strainer and let it drain into a large plastic pitcher.

RASPBERRY SHRUB

1 cup (125 g) fresh raspberries   1 cup (200 g) white sugar
1 cup (240 ml) cold water   1 cup (240 ml) white vinegar

Combine all the ingredients in the bowl of a food processor or blender and puree. Strain through a fine-mesh sieve into a nonreactive container. Store airtight in the refrigerator for up to three months.

From Neal Bodenheimer and Emily Timberlake, Cure: New Orleans Drinks and How to Mix 'Em *(2022). Used by permission.*

Even after straining, the fresh shrub remained frothy and foamy. The reason, Bodenheimer explained, is that raspberries contain a lot of pectin. "If you want a really snappy, lighter highball," he added, "you should try and get the pectin out." He noted that a lot of old raspberry shrub recipes call for cooking and skimming the mixture to remove the pectin as it rises to the top.

But not for the Roffignac. "For this drink, the pectin actually helps," he said. "It's nice because it gives it mouth feel and richness. Most long drinks don't get a lot of that."

The shrub ready, Bodenheimer set out to mix up some Roffignacs. He started with an Armagnac one, which is the spirit he uses in the house version at Cure and in the bar's cocktail book. He scooped four ice cubes into a tall collins glass, then set it aside and picked up a cocktail shaker. Into the shaker went a few ice cubes, then a jigger of Armagnac followed by a pony of the pink shrub. He snapped the lid onto the shaker, gave it a quick three-second shake, then poured the contents, which now had a peachy pink glow, into the glass and topped it with soda water.

"I think the fruit and the fruit distillate play really well together," Bodenheimer said, as he set the tall glass in front of me on the bar.

I took a sip and agreed. It was a bright drink, with a little candylike sweetness and a pleasant fizz. The Armagnac bite was there, but it lurked in the background as a sort of muted base note.

CURE'S ROFFIGNAC

1½ ounces (45 ml) Darroze 8-Year "Les Grands Assemblages" Bas-Armagnac

1 ounce (30 ml) raspberry shrub

Soda water, to top

Fresh raspberries, for garnish

Combine the Armagnac and shrub in a cocktail shaker filled with ice and shake until chilled. Double-strain into a collins glass filled with ice and top with the soda water. Garnish with the fresh raspberries and serve.

From Neal Bodenheimer and Emily Timberlake, Cure: New Orleans Drinks and How to Mix 'Em *(2022). Used by permission.*

From there, we set about exploring various permutations and combinations, all with the same proportions of spirit, shrub, and soda, but with different liquors and different ways of blending. "If I didn't shake it and I just stirred, it'd be a different drink," Bodenheimer said. To prove the point, he took a bottle of French brandy and this time built the drink in the glass, stirring the brandy and shrub together before adding four cubes of ice and two ounces of soda.

It was indeed a different drink, darker in color and much boozier and brandy forward. "I like that one a lot," I said.

Before long, a half dozen glasses were lined up along the bar, their contents varying in hue from rosy pink to pale orange depending on the darkness of the spirit. We tried pisco, Louisiana rum, and then, in a nod to what we supposed was historical accuracy, rye whiskey.

"Ugh. This is harsh," I exclaimed after my first sip. The flavors fought like cats in a sack.

"It's just doesn't taste good," Bodenheimer agreed. "It's not the stuff you want."

For the rye Roffignac, Bodenheimer had selected a

bottle of Sazerac, which is distilled in Kentucky and is a so-called "low rye" whiskey. That means around 51 percent of the grain that went into the still was rye and the rest a blend of corn and malted barley. "Most of the ryes that we carry [at Cure] are going be in that Kentucky style," Bodenheimer said, "where they're a little richer, fuller—like kind of the missing link between rye and bourbon."

I suspect, though, that even a 95 percent "high rye" mash bill would lead to a similar result, for what's clashing with the fruity sweetness of the raspberry shrub is not the basic flavor of the grains but all the sweet and spicy notes—vanilla, caramel, pepper, ginger—that the whiskey takes on from long aging in charred oak barrels.

For me, the clear winner of the taste test was the version made with a spirit completely unknown to local residents when old New Orleans was young: tequila. For that one, Bodenheimer selected Arette Blanco, one of the few tequilas that's still made in the Mexican town of Tequila. It has definite floral notes that blend quite nicely with the sweet, fruity shrub.

"That's one you could sell a lot of on a hot day," I said after my first taste. "Maybe even serve it over crushed ice."

Bodenheimer also ranked the tequila version at the top. "Given how people feel about tequila these days," he said, "I think a tequila or mescal Roffignac is a very easy choice, because tequila and raspberry, they love each other."

So there you have it. A tequila Roffignac. Joseph Roffignac, we should note, *did* serve in the Dragoons of Mexico before moving to New Orleans.

THE JOSÉ ROFFIGÑAC

1½ ounces (45 ml) Arette Blanco or other white tequila
1 ounce (30 ml) raspberry shrub
Soda water, to top
Fresh raspberries, for garnish

Combine the tequila and shrub in a cocktail shaker filled with ice and shake until chilled. Double-strain into a fancy glass filled with crushed ice, and top with the soda water. Garnish with fresh raspberries and serve.

I think it's even better with a squeeze of lime, since tequila and lime love each other, too.

GETTING HISTORICAL

Neal Bodenheimer's approach is to be inspired by the history of a cocktail but not be bound by it. He uses the original recipe less as a formula and more as a framework for creating a modern interpretation. As bartenders, he reminded me, "our job is to make things that taste good, and that people want to drink. You can never forget that."

As a historian, though, I wanted to know how the original version might have tasted and why people might have embraced it. Back home in Charleston, I built off our experiments in New Orleans, as well as the archival research I had done, and undertook to create a historically accurate version of the Roffignac.

It was not an easy thing to do. As we have seen, no recipe from before Prohibition survives. We can glean a sense of the ingredients from various nineteenth-century accounts, but the versions of those ingredients we have today are hardly the same as their counterparts just 150 years ago.

The first Roffignacs were made with whiskey, but what kind? It was unlikely to have been a smooth-sipping brown spirit like modern bourbon or rye. The practice of aging whiskey in charred oak barrels had not yet been adopted. Most of the whiskey on the market at the time was cheap, newly distilled white whiskey, though one could pay more for "old whiskey," which would have rested in regular un-charred barrels for several years after distilling. Time in the raw wood would have mellowed the harsh bite and perhaps given a pale golden hue to the spirits, but the end product would not have had the ruddy color nor the rich, complex flavors that are imparted by heavily charred oak.

Then there's the syrup. Most bartenders today make raspberry shrub with granulated white sugar, but the base ingredient for "sirup" just after the Civil War would have been loaf sugar. Even if a syrup maker added egg whites and boiled and skimmed their sugar to clarify it, the finished product would surely have retained some of the darker notes of molasses.

Here's an even thornier question: would that infamous nineteenth-century Roffignac syrup have been flavored by raspberries or raspberry vinegar? The earliest accounts note just "whiskey syrup" or "Roffignac syrup" with no mention of other flavorings. No source from before Prohibition makes any reference to raspberry in connection with the Roffignac. Was *himbeeressig,* as Stanley C. Arthur asserted, actually used "when old New Orleans was young," or was that a twentieth-century adaptation?

Faced with all these uncertainties, here's where I landed. Instead of straight bourbon or rye whiskey, which by law must be aged at least two years in new charred oak barrels, I went with Mellow Corn Straight Corn Whiskey, which is aged for four years in used bourbon barrels. That makes it a lighter, straw-colored spirit, and at 100 proof, it certainly packs a punch.

My hypothesis was that the "whiskey syrup" mentioned in nineteenth-century accounts of the Roffignac would not simply be a whiskey-flavored syrup but rather a dose of spirits mixed with sugar syrup and some sort of flavoring to mask the whiskey taste. That flavoring may well have been raspberry, for in that 1892 *Mascot* sketch, the jag-ridden son orders a Roffignac and the father a raspberry soda. Furthermore, if people in the early twentieth century were using *himbeeressig* in their Roffignacs, then it seems a good bet that the original may have had a little vinegary zip, too. So, I decided to make a raspberry vinegar syrup following the recipe in Christian Schultz's 1862 *Manual for the Manufacture of Cordials, Liquor, Fancy Syrups, & c.* I did scale down the ingredients, though, since Schultz's version calls for thirty pounds of raspberries, seven and a half gallons of cider vinegar, and eighty pounds of sugar, which by my estimate would generate enough raspberry vinegar syrup to supply the entire United States for several years of Roffignac-making.

For the sugar, I went with demerara, a tan-colored "raw" sugar that is less processed than regular white sugar and still has traces of molasses. Turbinado or other raw cane sugars would be similar in flavor, too.

HIMBEERESSIG

8 ounces fresh raspberries (frozen will do in a pinch)
2 cups cider vinegar

Put the raspberries and vinegar in a large glass jar or other nonreactive container and allow to rest unrefrigerated for at least eight days. Strain vinegar through a fine mesh sieve lined with cheesecloth into a bowl, pressing down on the solids to extract all the juice. Store in a bottle or glass jar until ready to use.

HIMBEERESSIG SYRUP

1 cup Himbeeressig (see recipe above)
1 cup demerara or other raw sugar

Combine the himbeeressig and sugar in a saucepan and bring almost to a boil over high heat, stirring until the sugar is dissolved. Remove from the stove and allow to cool, then pour into a bottle or jar. Store in the refrigerator if you don't plan to use the same day.

Finally, there was the question of ice. From early on, ice was used inside the soda fountain apparatus to chill the fizzy water before it was dispensed, but it doesn't appear that ice was regularly put in the serving glasses until the 1890s. By that point, mechanical freezers had made ice less expensive, and ice shavers became standard soda fountain equipment.

Every Roffignac recipe I've seen calls for the drink to be served over ice cubes or crushed ice, but would the ones at Lopez's Confectionery or Soda McCloskey's have been served cold from the fountain with no ice in the glass? I suspect that they would have. Fortunately, we don't need ice today to chill our soda water, for we have refrigerators.

With these parameters in mind, I set out to recreate a nineteenth-century Roffignac. The goal was not to discover a delicious cocktail that one might serve with pride in an upscale bar. Instead, I was trying to come up with something that would be refreshing and look right at home being served alongside a raspberry soda or root beer at a soda fountain. More than anything, I didn't want it to taste too boozy, for the whole point of a Roffignac was to hide the whiskey, not accentuate it.

It took some doing. That himbeeressig syrup on its own is delicious—sweet but tangy, with a dark rich flavor from the demerara sugar—but a little goes a long way in a drink. My first take, which used the same 3:2 ratio as Neil Bodenheimer's Roffignacs (1½ ounces of whiskey to 1 ounce syrup), was a tart punch to the mouth—far too vinegary. As I dialed back the syrup and upped the ratio to 2:1 then 3:1, the drink improved, but it also got a lot boozier. So, I began cutting the himbeeressig with demerara simple syrup (a 1:1 mix of sugar and water) and ended up with a beverage that seemed, to my taste buds, at least, almost a soft drink.

The soda water's fizziness made it quite refreshing on a hot summer day. The sweetness of the sugar and tart bite of vinegar didn't erase the whiskey flavor, necessarily, but it certainly dampened it. I took a sip here and a sip there as I was cleaning up the prodigious mess on my kitchen counter. It went down easy. Then all of a sudden I realized my cheeks were tingling and my brain was a little fuzzy. That whiskey had snuck right up and taken hold. Feet-tangling powers, indeed.

THE ACTUAL ORIGINAL (PERHAPS) ROFFIGNAC COCKTAIL

1½ ounces Mellow Corn or unaged rye whiskey

⅔ ounce demerara simple syrup (made from 1 part demerara sugar to 1 part water)

⅓ ounce himbeeressig syrup (see recipe above)

Chilled soda water to taste

Combine the whiskey and syrups in an 8-ounce soda glass and stir. Fill to top with chilled soda water and give one final stir.

Could this be the original Roffignac? It's possible—but I wouldn't bet real money on it.

AFTERWORD

THE FUTURE OF THE ROFFIGNAC

So where will the Roffignac go from here? On one front, its prospects seem rosy. In the past few years it has managed to do something it never pulled off during its heyday at the turn of the twentieth century: venture outside of New Orleans.

In 2021, Neal Bodenheimer brought the Roffignac to Washington, D.C., when he and his partners opened Dauphine's, a New Orleans–themed restaurant five blocks north of the White House. There, however, he took the liberty of using tequila instead of brandy or whiskey as the base spirit, and he made the shrub from cranberries instead of raspberries. "In D.C. it was very important for us to keg a drink," he explained to me. "And the pectin level in the raspberries was so high. When you put carbonation into it, it just goes *phhsssst*. It explodes. It was like a very, very, very foamy substance when we kegged it, so we switched it to a cranberry Roffignac."

When New Orleans natives Miles and Alex Pincus opened their nautical-themed bar, Holywater, in Lower Manhattan in 2022, their drinks menu offered a selection of classic New Orleans cocktails, alongside New York specialties. The New Orleans list included a Roffignac made along more standard lines, with cognac, raspberry shrub, lemon, and seltzer—and priced at a cool $21.

As I write this final chapter, though, the waters seem to have gotten a bit choppier for the revived cocktail. It's one thing to bring back a long-lost drink and convince guests to give it a try. It's another thing to get them to order a second one—much less make it their go-to drink.

Cocktails writer Robert Simonson was not exactly bowled over when he sampled the recently revived Roffignac at the Chandelier Bar in 2022. "Whether it needed rescuing, I'm still not convinced," he wrote in his Substack newsletter *The Mix.* "It tasted overwhelmingly of raspberry, as Roffignacs tend to."

As of this writing, the Roffignac is no longer on the menu at Holywater in New York, and its place in the "N.O.L.A." section is now filled by a classic Sazerac. Chris Hannah will happily mix you a Roffignac at the Jewel of the South, if you ask for one, as will Neal Bodenheimer at Cure. It's not currently on the regular menu at either bar, though.

As we wrapped up our Roffignac tasting session at Cure, I asked Bodenheimer whether he thought bartenders and cocktail fans would continue to embrace the drink. He was optimistic. "I think the Roffignac is an old cocktail format that's kind of ripe for rediscovering," he told me. "You could take raspberries, you could take different things. There's just a lot that can be done with the format of shrub, booze, and soda, right?"

He noted another virtue. "We talk a lot about juice waste in the world of beverages," he says. "If you think about the Roffignac, it's shrub, charged water, and spirit.

It's a very green cocktail, or it can be, because you could end up using it to process waste."

"If you're trying to do historical reproduction," he added, "I think that's a different game. If you're trying to make a drink taste good that's inspired by the Roffignac, then I think the sky is the limit."

For me, the Roffignac serves more as a cautionary tale for bartenders, drinks writers, and cocktail enthusiasts. We are all driven by the very human need for stories. A well-made drink sipped by itself with no context might taste pretty good, but it's going to taste even better if it has an appealing name and the bartender can spin you a compelling yarn while shaking or stirring it up. In crafting those tales, though, we have a natural tendency to project the modern world onto the past. We fill in the missing details with our own preconceptions of how things must have been or with something that simply sounds good.

As slippery as it is, cocktail history is still very valuable. Neal Bodenheimer found in the Roffignac a format that he can adapt to create an array of interesting and tasty new beverages, even if they use completely different ingredients and are served in totally different ways. I found in the Roffignac a window into New Orleans dining and drinking history that dragged me away from the well-worn footrails of coffeehouses and saloons and into places I might not otherwise have visited—soda fountains, confectionery shops, and old Creole restaurants struggling to survive as the city eased toward the twenty-first century.

The chase, in other words, has value in and of itself, even if in the end your quarry manages to slip away.

RESOURCES

BOOKS

Arthur, Stanley Clisby. *Famous New Orleans Drinks & How to Mix 'Em*. 1937. Rpt. Gretna, LA: Pelican Publishing Company, 2011.

Bodenheimer, Neal, and Emily Timberlake. *Cure: New Orleans Drinks and How to Mix 'Em*. New York: Abrams, 2022.

Castellanos, Henry C. *New Orleans as It Was: Episodes of Louisiana Life*. 1895. Rpt. Baton Rouge: Louisiana State University Press, 1978.

Funderburg, Anne Cooper. *Sundae Best: A History of Soda Fountains*. Bowling Green, OH: Bowling Green State University Popular Press, 2002.

Kendall, John. *History of New Orleans*. Chicago: Lewis, 1922.

King, Grace Elizabeth. *Creole Families of New Orleans*. New York: Macmillan, 1921.

Laborde, Peggy Scott, and Tom Fitzmorris. *Lost Restaurants of New Orleans*. Gretna, LA: Pelican, 2011.

Laborde, Peggy Scott and John Magill. *Canal Street: New Orleans' Great Wide Way*. Gretna: Pelican, 2006.

Schultz, Christian. *Manual for the Manufacture of Cordials, Liquors, Fancy Syrups, & c*. New York: Dick & Fitzgerald, 1876.

Taistro, Louis Fitzgerald. *Random Shots and Southern Breezes*. New York: Harper and Brothers, 1842.

Thomas, Jerry. *How to Mix Drinks, or The Bon-Vivant's Companion.* New York: Dick & Fitzgerald, 1862.

Washburne, George R., and Stanley Bronner. *Beverages De Luxe.* 2nd Edition. Louisville, KY: Wine and Spirits Bulletin, 1914.

Wondrich, David, and Noah Rothbaum, ed. *The Oxford Companion to Spirits and Cocktails.* New York: Oxford University Press, 2022.

ARTICLES

Din, Gilbert C. "A Troubled Seven Years: Spanish Reactions to American Claims and Aggression in 'West Florida,' 1803–1810." *Louisiana History* 59:4 (2018): 409–52.

Gayarré, Charles. "A Street in Old New Orleans." *American Magazine* 7 (1887): 155–64.

"He Fooled His Father." *The Mascot,* No. 54 (July 2, 1892): 8.

Karst, James. "The Cocktail Named for a New Orleans Mayor—or was it?" *Times-Picayune* (July 23, 2016).

Laborde, Errol. "Roffignac—The Mayor and The Cocktail." *New Orleans* (October 7, 2019).

Pearce, Elizabeth. "New Orleans' Other Poison." *Saveur* (January 5, 2015). www.saveur.com/article/wine-and-drink/new-orleans-cocktail -roffignac. Accessed August 3, 2022.

"Those Eyes." *New Orleans Picayune.* Rpt. *Zion's Home Monthly* 3 (1894): 540–42.

Tyrrell, Ian R. "Drink and Temperance in the Antebellum South: An Overview and Interpretation." *Journal of Southern History* 48 (November 1982): 485–510.

THESIS

Jarrett, Mindy. "'Drinking' about the Past: Bar Culture in Antebellum New Orleans." MA Thesis, University of New Orleans (December 2018).

ICONIC NEW ORLEANS COCKTAILS

The Sazerac

The Café Brûlot

The Vieux Carré

The Absinthe Frappé

The Roffignac